NOT ME

Eileen Myles

Looking Back at the End of the World
**JEAN BAUDRILLARD, GUNTER GEBAUER,
DIETMAR KAMPER, DIETER LENZEN,
EDGAR MORIN, GERBURG TREUSCH-DIETER
PAUL VIRILIO & CHRISTOPH WULF**

Foucault Live
MICHEL FOUCAULT

Forget Foucault
JEAN BAUDRILLARD

Behold Metaron, The Recording Angel
SOL YURICK

Bolo'Bolo
P. M.

Speed & Politics
PAUL VIRILIO

On the Line
GILLES DELEUZE & FÉLIX GUATTARI

Sadness at Leaving
ERJE AYDEN

Remarks on Marx
MICHEL FOUCAULT

69 Ways to Sing the Blues
JÜRG LAEDERACH

Interventions
MICHEL FOUCAULT

Assassination Rhapsody
DEREK PELL

Communists Like Us
FÉLIX GUATTARI & TONY NEGRI

Germania
HEINER MÜLLER

NOT ME

Eileen Myles

SEMIOTEXT(E)

Some of these poems have appeared in the following publications: *Shiny, GEM, Blue Smoke, The World, B-City, Between C & D, The Little Magazine, City 9, The Baltimore Sun Magazine, Oink, The Poetry Project Newsletter, Nice to See You, Paris Review, Bomb, Best American Poetry 1988, American Letters and Commentary, Big Scream 26, Ploughshares, The Brooklyn Review, Cover, Pome, Forehead, Mirage, Cuz, New Leaves Review, The National Poetry Magazine of the Lower East Side, Poets for Life, Mudfish, Broadway, Outlook, Bombay Gin* and *The Santa Monica Review*.

«How I Wrote Certain of My Poems»
first appeared in *Cuz* as «Hot Night Part II».

The poems in *Not Me* were written in 1986-1989.
The Real Drive was written in 1981-85.

The author wishes to thank Joan Larkin, David Trinidad, Tim Dlugos, Alice Notley, David Rattray, Susie Timmons, Jimmy Schuyler, Tom Carey, Kate Lambert, Chris Kraus and Sylvère Lotringer for their friendship, insight and support.

Design & Text Production: Kim Spurlock @ Art&Language
Photo: Bob Berg

Semiotext(e)
P O Box 629
South Pasadena, CA 91031

Printed in the United States of America
978-0-936756-67-7 (pb. : alk. paper)
We gratefully acknowledge
financial assistance in the
publication of this book from the
New York State Council on the Arts.

10 9 8 7 6 5

FOR MYRA MNIEWSKI

CONTENTS

NOT ME

AN AMERICAN POEM

I was born in Boston in
1949. I never wanted
this fact to be known, in
fact I've spent the better
half of my adult life
trying to sweep my early
years under the carpet
and have a life that
was clearly just mine
and independent of
the historic fate of
my family. Can you
imagine what it was
like to be one of them,
to be built like them,
to talk like them
to have the benefits
of being born into such
a wealthy and powerful
American family. I went
to the best schools,
had all kinds of tutors
and trainers, travelled
widely, met the famous,
the controversial, and
the not-so-admirable
and I knew from
a very early age that
if there were ever any
possibility of escaping

the collective fate of this famous
Boston family I would
take that route and
I have. I hopped
on an Amtrak to New
York in the early
'70s and I guess
you could say
my hidden years
began. I thought
Well I'll be a poet.
What could be more
foolish and obscure.
I became a lesbian.
Every woman in my
family looks like
a dyke but it's really
stepping off the flag
when you become one.
While holding this ignominious
pose I have seen and
I have learned and
I am beginning to think
there is no escaping
history. A woman I
am currently having
an affair with said
you know you look
like a Kennedy. I felt
the blood rising in my
cheeks. People have
always laughed at
my Boston accent

confusing «large» for
«lodge,» «party»
for «potty.» But
when this unsuspecting
woman invoked for
the first time my
family name
I knew the jig
was up. Yes, I am,
I am a Kennedy.
My attempts to remain
obscure have not served
me well. Starting as
a humble poet I
quickly climbed to the
top of my profession
assuming a position of
leadership and honor.
It is right that a
woman should call
me out now. Yes,
I am a Kennedy.
And I await
your orders.
You are the New Americans.
The homeless are wandering
the streets of our nation's
greatest city. Homeless
men with AIDS are among
them. Is that right?
That there are no homes
for the homeless, that
there is no free medical

help for these men. And *women*.
That they get the message
—as they are dying—
that this is not their home?
And how are your
teeth today? Can
you afford to fix them?
How high is your rent?
If art is the highest
and most honest form
of communication of
our times and the young
artist is no longer able
to move here to speak
to her time...Yes, I could,
but that was 15 years ago
and remember—as I must
I am a Kennedy.
Shouldn't we all be Kennedys?
This nation's greatest city
is home of the business-
man and home of the
rich artist. People with
beautiful teeth who are not
on the streets. What shall
we do about this dilemma?
Listen, I have been educated.
I have learned about Western
Civilization. Do you know
what the message of Western
Civilization is? I am alone.
Am I alone tonight?
I don't think so. Am I

the only one with bleeding gums
tonight. Am I the only
homosexual in this room

tonight. Am I the only
one whose friends have
died, are dying now.
And my art can't
be supported until it is
gigantic, bigger than
everyone else's, confirming
the audience's feeling that they are
alone. That they alone
are good, deserved
to buy the tickets
to see this Art.
Are working,
are healthy, should
survive, and are
normal. Are you
normal tonight? Everyone
here, are we all normal.
It is not normal for
me to be a Kennedy.
But I am no longer
ashamed, no longer
alone. I am not
alone tonight because
we are all Kennedys.
And I am your President.

EDWARD THE CONFESSOR

I have a confession to make
I wish there were
some role in society
I could fulfill
I could be a confessor

I have a confession to make

I have this way when I step
into the bakery on 2nd Ave.
of wanting to be the only
really nice person in the store
so the harried sales woman
with several toned hair
will like me. I do this in all
kinds of stores, coffee shops
xerox shops, everywhere I go.
And invariably I leave my keys,
xeroxing, my coffee
from the last place
I am being so nice. I try
so hard to make a great
impression on these neutral
strangers right down to
the perfect warm smile
I get entirely lost and
stagger back out onto
the street, bereft
of something major.
It's really leaning
too hard on the everyday.
My mother was
the kind of woman who
dragging us into stores
always seemed to charm the pants
off the cashier. She was such
a great person, so human

though at home she was
such a bitch, I mean really
distant. I imitate her and
I don't do it well. She didn't
leave her wallet
or us in a store.
I'm just a pale imitation
it is simply not my style
to open the hearts of
strangers to my true
personhood. I hope you accept
this tiny confession of what
I am currently going through.
And if you are experiencing
something of similar nature
tell someone, *not me,*
but tell someone. It's the new
human program to be in. It would
be nice for at least
these final moments if
we could sigh
with the relief
of being in
the same program
with all the
other humans
whispering
in school. I can't quite locate
the terror, but I am trying
to be my mother
or Edward the Confessor
smiling down on you with up-praying
hands. I am looking down at the
tips of my boots as I step
across the balcony of the
church excited to be allowed
to say these things. Outside my church
is a relationship. On 11th street
this guy and this woman are selling

the woman so they can
get more dope. All their things
are there, rags and loaves of
bread and make-up.
And there was—
this was incredible.
Two men lying by the door
of the church giving
each other blow-jobs.
They were sort of street
guys, one black one white.
I said hey you can't do
that here. They jumped
up, one spit come
out of his mouth. If you don't
get out of here I'll call
the cops. Don't call the
cops we'll go, we'll leave.

That was a shock. That was more
than I expected to see in
a day. Something about
seeing the guy spit
come out of his
mouth. He didn't
have to do that.
I guess I scared
him. I couldn't
believe my eyes.
I was scared too.

EVERYTHING'S HOUSE

I mix my grapes with
your grapes and the
plate's too small &
my grapes go bouncing
on the floor. The bounce
of three or four grapes.
Before, when I parked
my bike onto some
orange construction
they built around
the regular street
sign so like
the forest
you couldn't see
it's top.
I started unlocking
my bike with the
keys to your
house I was
so excited to
be coming here.
It was a funny
day. For once
I experienced
the pain of
the pavement,
black pizza
face with
metal squares
leaning on one
another like
the street's
been hurt
by NYU &

has a plate
or a cast. And
then it's gouged,
& puckered, laid
bare & violated
gradually persuaded
into sidewalk
but the street
must know the
city is taking care
of it, right?
The canes of
old folks tapping
on its back. Babies
being wheeled for
a few months. Bikes
(me) bouncing off
sidewalks & onto
it breaking turning
going the wrong
way, Free.

When I came
in I switched
on the light
to a yellow &
black striped
towel on the
floor & a big
smashed water-
melon & a
pair of
cowboy boots.
I love your
life. You must
have taken
a bath. But

I must stay
in my life
now. Taking
my drops
like that
pot in the
sink.

Most of your
grapes are
gone & mine
are dusty &
warm, need
to be washed.
Yours are
over-ripe &
so I'm really
saving them
by eating them
now. Why is
everything sold
at the wrong
temperature
except
clothes.
I eat
the warm
loose grapes
because I
really have
a problem,
the wrong
streets the
wrong city,
& my god
your flowers
died! I

can't even
tell what
they were!
Were they
tulips. I think
they were tulips.
I can't believe
I haven't been
here for
so long that
those beautiful
tulips died.

I love this
kind of
poetry: your
building re-
minds me of
my first
apartment.
People playing
musical instru-
ments & stereos
playing too
loud. Human
insanity. I
never feel
lonely this
way. My
building passed
through this
phase six
years ago.
By now
everyone's
jowelly
& settled in

from word-
processing.
And look
at that!
All that
expensive
new under-
wear still
exactly on
the couch
from when
you bought
it. The big
lavender un-
derpants
on top. Gentian
undies. Waves
of boiling water
on its way
to being my
tea so it
can really
be night.

                    Oh
god what
if you
don't come
home. Or what
if you just
come in
really late
& go *oh*
You bought
lemons
too.
    Yeah

but I'm
going to
bring mine
home you
have so
many. We'll
use them
you say.
I'd like
it better
if you'd
come &
visit
them at
my house. How
do we live
in houses in
the middle
Of New
York City.
Eileen Myles
born in
a house
died in
a house.
The embarrassments,
the futility,
the neighbor's
flight on
her clarinet,
every car door
slam, baby
it's you
but I
know you're
on a bike.

When the time
comes to
stop I'll
have stopped
already so
many times
I won't
know how
to wind
down. Good
night Eileen.
No, but. Eileen,
you've said
it all. I don't
think you
understand.
I meant
to leave
when I
was 30!
Why didn't
I go
to Europe.
I couldn't
believe in
God because
I don't
feel taken
care of.
She's down-
stairs play-
ing a
clarinet.

I don't
speak
another
language.

Die in
English
then. Oh,
now—I
can even
hear the
clock
I'm so
peaceful. Isn't
it fast. That's
your time. Don't
tell me death's
so much
like life.

Honey I'm home.

You do it
different
all the time.
You spread
your keys
differently.
You gloat
at what
you get
when that
wasn't
what
they wanted
at all.

You don't
say things
to people
because
you don't

want to
make them
feel bad
when it's
just your
conceit. You're
all alone
except
when you
think of
them. Desperately.
Talking with
yourself. Wishing
they would
come back or
go away or
something. The
people, the
humans, God.

I have
never been
so bothered
by a human
being before.
Let me screw
the cap on
the seltzer.
I could
have gone
out on
you tonight.
I imagined
you furious.
But I
was so
angry

I didn't
feel a
thing. Just
the breeze
on my
chin. The
bike bouncing
on the
pavement.
My boredom
with life.
If some-
thing is
taking
care of
me & all
of us
it better
hold us
tight
& not
say a
word.
It better
love me
me tonight
for saying
these words
for it. If
the birds
get away
with what
they do,
and time
passes. I
lean my
hip on the

window
ledge,
I'm 36.

If I
ever thought
when I
moved in
I'd live
here for
nine years,
watching
my neighbors
get old.

And I
can't even
imagine
what it
must
be like
to die.

HOLES

Once when I passed East Fourth Street off First Avenue,
I think it was in early fall, and I had a small hole
in the shoulder of my white shirt, and another on
the back—I looked just beautiful. There was a
whole moment in the 70s when it was beautiful
to have holes in your shirts and sweaters.
By now it was 1981, but I carried that 70s style
around like a torch. There was a whole way of
feeling about yourself that was more European
than American, unless it was American around
1910 when it was beautiful to be a strong
starving immigrant who believed so much
in herself and she was part of a movement
as big as history and it explained the
hole in her shirt. It's the beginning
of summer tonight and every season has
cracks through which winter
or fall might leak out. The most perfect
flavor of it, oddly in June. Oh remember
when I was an immigrant. I took a black
beauty and got up from the pile of poems
around my knees and just had too much
energy for thought and walked over to
your house where there was continuous
beer. Finally we were just drinking
Rheingold, a hell of a beer. At the
door I mentioned I had a crush on both
of you, what you say to a couple. By
now the kids were in bed. I can't
even say clearly now that I wanted
the woman, though it seemed to be
the driving principle then, wanting
one of everything. I was part of
a generation of people who went to
bars on 7th street and drank the
cheap whiskey and the ale on tap and dreamed
about when I would get you alone. Those
big breasts. I carried slim notebooks which only
permitted two or three-word lines, I need you.
«Nearing the Horse.» There was blood in all my
titles, and milk. I had two bright blue pills
in my pocket. I loved you so much. It was
the last young thing I ever did, the end of
my renaissance, an immigration into my

dream world which even my grandparents
had not dared to live, being prisoners
of schizophrenia and alcohol, though
I was lovers with the two. The beauty
of the story is that it happened.
It was the last thing that happened
in New York. Everything else happened
while I was stopping it from happening.
Everything else had a life of
its own. I don't think I owe
them an apology, though at least
one of their kids hates my guts.
She can eat my guts for all
I care. I had a small hole in
the front of my black sleeveless
sweater. It was just something
that happened. It got larger
and larger. I liked to put
my finger in it. In the month
of December I couldn't get
out of bed. I kept waking
up at 6PM and it was Christmas
or New Year's and I had to
start drinking & eating. I remember
you handed me the most beautiful
red plate of pasta. It was like your cunt
on a plate. I met people in your house,
even found people to go out and fuck,
regrettably, not knowing about
the forbidden fruit. I forget
what the only sin is. Somebody
told me recently. I have so
many holes in my memory. Between
me and the things I'm separated
from. I pick up a book and
another book and memory
and separation seem to
be all anyone writes
about. Or all they
seem to let me read.
But I remember those
beautiful holes on
my back like a
beautiful cloak
of feeling.

I named
the thing I felt
as I was walking
down the street.
The scratchy voiced
woman yelling at
me looked like
Nude my high school
friend. Speak English
she yelled. Yeah
I yelled back
but I was thinking
of her ass on
the sidewalk
outside Gem
Spa. Ouch
she must
have a pretty
ragged asshole
you know with
the kind of
life she leads
but I didn't take
her home this
winter. I think
I will see the
poor everywhere
this year and
feel for them.
Is that a crime?
I hear Jimmy
a guy who
reminds me
of my Dad refer

to himself as
a guest of the City.
Who live in back
wards of Manhattan
State, shelters,
shitholes, sidewalks.
Behold the guests.
We must love them
with their sores,
their ragged
butts. You know
they dump the
men who
don't fit on 3rd
Street out on
Ward's Island.
I see those buses
outside the Men's
Shelter when
I mistakenly
walk up Third.
As a tourist of
other bad lives
I visited Carryl
at all sorts of
looney bins & hideaways.
The Church of the
American Witch
she says.
That's when I picked
up the information
about where the
mystery buses
go. Naturally
there are garbage
islands & human
garbage islands.

You can think
of those
golden buses
filled with stinking
men as scows.
I abhorred Dr. Williams'
self-proclaimed com-
passion for the
woman giving birth.
O sensitive man
getting lyrical about
her labor pains.
Every bit of human
garbage that lines
the stairs to the
subway this winter
shouldn't move
me. My boots
cost 300
bucks. I didn't
do the wrong
thing at the wrong
time I did
the right
thing. Part
of me
should live
in the
street
with the
bums &
my bleeding
broken heart.
Or perhaps
I should
be in a
helping profession

rather than
an observing
profession.
Love Saves
the Day where
Madonna
buys her
clothes. I
went back
to the
corner
and gave
her a
buck
for this
poem.

THE FACE

The other night
I spoke to you
on the phone
about the feet.
But the face
is so much more
astonishing.
It will be mine
all my life
and tell you
who I am.
With its mouth
and eyes.
It will express
disdain and
pleasure
with its nose.
Its nose is
its sex. It tries
to decide if it
likes you or
not. It does!
And now the eyes
can show it.
The eyes are embarrassed
they have been hurt
and they fear they
can be read, but
the face feels proud
and won't shut
its eyes   it cannot
be that obvious.
It can only hope.
The mouth goes:
are you kidding
I can't believe
you! and protrudes
and turns down.
The mouth thinks

you're great. It laughs
and shows teeth.
The mouth likes you.
The mouth sees you

and smiles. But the eyes
have been hurt and
now have to turn away
so the tears don't
show. That telling wetness.
The mouth has words
it has great words
but it is learning
not to speak all
the time
but to just
kind of watch.
And when it
knows,—how
will it know?
It will listen
with the ears.
It will stop listening
and think.
It will listen
to a great many
other mouths.
The ears are perhaps
closest to the
heart the way
the nose
has sex
and the eyes
have truth.
The face, it is
so good. It is
like a big
human lamp
a globe of love
yet it is so
capable of
cruelty.

My mother
turned 65
today. The
most beautiful
poet in the
universe is
her daughter.
Does she
know that?
Mom you
sound like
the world's
youngest
senior citizen.
She's just
giggling
with delight
at her
new senior
citizen's
bus pass
she got
this morn-
ing. She
sounds
like she's
waited
her whole
life for
a free
ride.

Mom, do
you use
that walk-
man, are
you using

that walk-
man? Oh
yes. Cause
I was thinking
I would
send you
something
No, no
she assures
in a
terrified
tone. You've
done *enough*
I just listen
to my
radio. That's
plenty,
no more
walk-
man stuff.
No thank
you. Where
are you
calling from.
Well this
is costing
you plenty.
This is
coming
out of
your budget.
Well this
has been
fine. This
has been
just enough.
Well, thank
you for
calling. Uh-
huh.

What's the two best smelling
things in the world?
The inside of my brief-
case
        and then this
        person I
            I know. The birds
        are screeching
        for attention
        today. Wind blowing
        boats down the
            street. People in
        leather back-
            packs talking
                about Chanel,
        my laundry *Plump*
        in my hand.
I can see you through
the grid of
    my life. A slight
distance, doing
    your things.
I want to go
    take your temperature
go to Russia
    with you.
    Look in your
    eyes, so
    foreign
    & blue. They look
like a couple of question
marks. I stand with
    my cup in my
hand, this
    day, while
    it's waiting
    for You.

Everything's
  so far away—
my jacket's
  over there. I'm terrified
   to go & you
won't miss me
  I'm terrified by the
bright blues of
   the subway
   other days I'm
   so happy &
prepared to believe
  that everyone walking
down the street is
   someone I know.
The oldness of Macy's
  impresses me. The
  wooden escalators
    as you get
higher up to the furniture,
  credit, lampshades—
   You shopped here
   as a kid. Oh,
  you deserve me! In
  a movie called
   Close Up—once in
a while the wiggly
bars, notice
  the wiggly blue
  bars of
   subway entrances,
the grainy beauty,
  the smudge. I won't
kill myself today. It's
  too beautiful. My heart
   breaking down 23rd

St. To share this
with you, the
sweetness of the
        frame. My body
in perfect shape
for nothing but
death. I want
to show you this.
        On St. Mark's Place
        a madman screams:
my footsteps, the
        drumbeats of Armageddon.
        Oh yes bring me
        closer to you Lord.
I want to die
        Close Up. A handful
of bouncing yellow
        tulips for David.   I
        admit I love tulips
            because they
        die so beautifully.
                                    I

        see salvation in
their hanging heads.
A beautiful exit. How do
        they get to
            feel so free? I am
        trapped by love—
            over french fries
        my eyes wander to
            The Hue Bar. A blue
        sign. Across the
life. On my way to
        making a point,
            to making
            logic, to not
falling in love to-
            night and
        let my pain remain

unwrapped—to push
the machine—Paul's
staying in touch, but
oh remember Jessica
Lange, she looked so
beautiful all
doped up, on her
way to meet King
Kong. I sit
on my little red
couch in February
how do they get
to feel so free
1,000,000 women
not me moving through
the street tonight
of this filmy
city & I
crown myself
again & again
and there
can't be
two kings.

AT LAST

EILEEN MYLES NOT ME AT LAST

I always fall in love with tired
women. It seems I have the
time. On the blackboard
at the Gay Community
Center it said:
Ladies, we need your
blood. Afterwards
come to the Women's
Coffee House and
have a cup of
coffee. Donation
$1.00. He won't
be complaining
about his big
toe that hurts.
The man who
died last
night. The Death
Squad has taken
him away. I thought
of all the clothes
that guy must've
had. Now no one
can stand to
wear them. I use
Central America
& Southeast
Asia to ease
my mind. Pauline
Kael says that's
squalid. We live
in a culture of
vanishing men.
What is the difference.
Vincent's big joke
is his five-year

membership to
a video club.
They got him on
the phone at the
hospital. He
didn't know
how to say
one year
would probably
do just fine.
Another
thin man does
a night club
act—he does
show tunes
to the horror
of his visiting
friends. He'll
take it on
the road once
he gets better.
At last he knows
what he wants
to do! Jimmy Wayne's
family says Well,
that's what you
get. But I get
something dif-
ferent. What I
do at my desk
is always different
from what I do
on my bed. I was
watching the dif-
ference last
week. This week
I'm different
again. Is it because
of windows that

I think the
day's square
and life is
shaped like
a train. The big
buds outside
my window
make me think
I'm outside
of life because
I can watch
her change
and she can't
see me. You'd
think I'd be
grateful for
my vision. It is
complex. A dance
of images gates
and branches
across buildings
statues windows
firescapes and
creeping cats.
Honey, life
is a blast
and I am
part of it
but you're
separate
from me.
It's how you
want it. The radio
starts up
and I nearly
lose my style.
I opened
my heart to
you and now

I feel like
an open wound.
I put my arms
around you
I thought
you felt
great. I called
it heaven
one day

disturbing
once the
train moved

now nothing's
the same.

after my fealty

is done to

you, Oh lady

I light

my candles

and I

croon

at the

moon

a tune

that is

your

name

HOT NIGHT

Hot night, wet night
you've seen me before.
When the streets are
drenched and shimmering
with themself, the
mangy souls that wan-
der & fascinate its
puddles, piles of
trash. Impersonal
street is a lover
to me—growling
thunder   lightning
to flash and light
up 7th as a little
mangy boy weaves
towards me &
laughing couples
kiss the puddles
with intended
sex in bright
shirts. It could
be another city
but it's this
city where
I start
being alone
& alive bringing
my candles
in while
I go walking
in the rain.
I think I
need a bowie
knife, a
pistol, a squealing
horn. You've

seen me before
hardly ever as
charged up as
now at the
end of my
rope by a
window in
the rain. July
is full of
pleasance, things
that can be
pushed to
fill to the
end of
the summer where
no one's ever
surprised to
have made it
to September
when something
lives—the
culture made
inside. In July
I am filled
with the death
of the streets,
you've seen
me before—
you're a wit-
ness to the
death of
my innocence
which came
teetering here
without ap-
petite. If
anything lives
I have seen
it in the street & why

am I falling in love
now with the old
& the scabrous. Why
am I giving my
money away. Sunday
I photographed mounds
of trash, finally
turned the focus on
me, a portrait I
could accept. I
feel erotic, oddly
magnetic to the
death of things
emptily attracted
to the available
empty space,
a step, or
I will not tell
you where I've
been but I
do & do not
belong. When the
dawn begins
I'm blue & lonesome
give me twilight
then the night,
let me be lost
in the lonesome
place, the human
sea of no one.
Drivel passes from
the mouths of
babes, smart shirts
bopping along,
art faces california
faces, the proud
march of culture
in New York City
Man are we buzzed

the screaming pork-
chops on the 4th
of July, the
disintegration of
the Hell's Angels,
can be loved,
now there are
10, can be
inclusive now
I smell death
everywhere. I hardly
think it's in me though
it always has been
my baby blossom,
I hope I make
it through the night
unplanned, nothing
dazzles me now,
who's driving? God?
I don't believe in
God. New notebook
I'm scared. My
hand tries to fly
free, but it's my
life, not my
death. Make
an inventory of
your occupations
remember now
there is sugar
in your coffee
and the band
will catch
you if you
fall. Remember,
remember—what
were Hart Crane's
last words—you
read them in

the Strand. My
dear—I've simply
disgraced myself.
You know a
genius when you've
seen one, don't
you. I'm one.
Take a good look,
you've seen me
before. Don't
turn back. Isn't
it a famous image
of the end of
Love, the famous
ride on the ferry.
Departing from
Land the Love, the
famous prow parting
the water now
as I jab my hand
inside you now
and churn. My bike
falls apart. The chain
collapses, the brakes
stuck, the wheel
wiggles, taking in-
ventory of my
teeth if they do
not look like
they will make
the long haul
I will leave
with them. My
poetry is here
for the haul,
the lonely woman's
tool—we have
tools now, we
have words &

lists, we have
real tears now,
absence, rage &
missing you is
not possible in
the New York
rain because
your name
is caught between
the drops &
I might throw
up, I can't
because it is
not beautiful
& I'm a
ward of the
state. Silly
children in
hats, raving
junkies, so
what, discreet
children, bad
songs, where's
the art? My
drivel in
the rain, or
the la-la-
the tape. I have
no hope for
my culture now.
It prefers fictions
over journals, it
doesn't want
my lives so
I choose streets
like a billionaire,
prove my coffee
counts. I
pick up "you" like

my midnight
rattle I shake
at the devil
of the night
that does not
scare me. It's
true I've done
nothing right
but I'm driven
by the rainbows
of trash in
puddles, the
frames posters,
& windows, the
marked sidewalks,
stray shoes,
can you imagine
selling used magazines,
poetry books on
a blanket, click,
dividing my time
by the tables, the
walks, 27, going
oh, oh, what
pain I need
whiskey sex
and I get
it.

age

consumable

pleasures of East Village

Everyone's nude
in the window
at Barney's
today. Is
that the idea?
Some are stretched
out on the floor,
others standing
with fingers
poised, backs
to us, slabs
of shiny
duct tape
on their
ass. Everyone
on the side-
walk seems
excited like
they're seeing
something
new. Remember
that Wednesday
night, Honey?
We were just
walking by. It
was like flipping
on the tube
the night Oswald
got shot. Naked
summer was upon
us. Not that hippy
kind of naked. Naked
like the end of the
century. Pale rose
white people naked.
Black people will

look great with
that nice chocolate
brown naked. There's
so much traffic. The
whole city seems empty
of love, just work
work, work. Bags under
everyone's eyes, packages
under their arms, the
day after Macy's big
sale and the blood
lust still upon them.
The art world slows
down in summer. Time
to go to the library
and find out what
it was. Gorky, who
was Gorky. Nancy Graves
seems like someone
smart and in all
hopeless little
clubs everyone
who ever waited
on me seems to
have been gay
for years. I am
so off. Everyone's
going away someplace
or just came back.
Somewhere everyone
is naked, just
for a little
bit. I never
seem to be
naked with you.
You were either
gone for too
long, or the
job's half done

and you're
tugging on
your clothes.
I would die
for sex and that's
my problem. It's
slowly happening
to the men I know
and I would like
to climb naked
on a cross
and die for
my sins
because
I've never
had enough.
It's time
for a female
Jesus. A naked
woman who knows
the score. We don't
have to do it because
she paid for us. She
says she paid for
us, and everyone
snickers. I gave
her fifty dollars
last night. She will not
leave me alone. I wish she'd
get a job. She's been doing
the same thing for so
long. You know she's
the same as she was
when she was drunk. No
different. She can't get
anything together. All
she cares about is her
body. She thinks everyone
is looking at her. Who

let her in! Self-
indulgent pain in the
ass. Some woman from
out-of-town throws
an empty bottle of Rolling
Rock at me. Some
woman I used to tie
up slugs me in the
face. A performance
troupe comes over and
spits on me. I hate
you, you're such a
scum bag! screams some-
one I used to like
a lot. Look, she
loves it, laughs
my sister. Eileen,
just get down,
says my mother.
I'm going home
to watch teevee.
We still think
you're a poet
not a performance
artist. It's not
like they make
any money. I
don't think there's
any funding for this
kind of work. See,
I always knew she
was like this. I'd
fuck her. In fact,
I already have. Eileen,
it's a great idea,
but we've got to
go get something
to eat. Are you
coming. I'll call

you tonight. Thanks
for inviting me.
Yeah, keep me
on your list.
I don't know,
I think you're
«doing something.»
It's very raw. Yeah,
she's got a lot
of nerve. Well, where
should we eat? Round
the clock? No—
their salads
are awful! Well then
you pick the
place. Okay,
Okay, Round the
clock. We don't
have to. *It's*
alright. Really!

Maybe this wasn't
such a good idea.
And the place
is a mess and *I've*
got to clean up.
Excuse me. Someone's
passed out on one of
those little tables.
Excuse me, could you
undo one of my feet
and a hand? I can
probably do the
rest. Yes, it's
me that's talking.
Up here on the
stage. The one
on the cross.

A BLUE JAY

They told
me to
meditate
so I pretended
I was waiting
in a Doctor's
office. You
can always
pick up
a magazine
National Geographic
go to
China,
but I'm
here &
the breezes
admit it.
Some birds
sound like
scratching
not singing
but I
believe
that's
how
they sing.

Once travelling
across America
I watched
my plane's
shadow
fall over
trees. I
felt evil.
Who wants

to watch
themselves
travel,
darkening
the land.

But if
I find
myself
cast in
someone else's
purposes
I feel free,
the one
who doesn't.
All I have
to do is
not step
on a bee
& I won't
get hurt.
At work
I don't
want to
do it &
here—
it's hard
to be
at peace.
This is
a song
to that.
I'm sorry
if it
sounds like
scratching.
Now, there's
nothing wrong
with a

tree over-
hanging a
lawn,
making a
shadow,
making
noise. You
might say
it belongs.
So does
that yellow
lawn chair.
If my
discomfort
continues
you'll see
where I
am. What
I have
on. Let's
say I'm
clothed
in Nature
w/ an
open ear.
Any more
riddles for
the human
race while
I've got
you here.
There's
a hollow
in the
trees. A
bush I
could crawl
in and
pee. The

trees are
my friends.
Hello Tree.
Can I come
out to a
tree. I know
you'd hardly
know it
to look at
me, but
would you
believe I'm
a Lesbian. But
Nature is
no stage.
Scaffolding of
hair itches
my nose. Those
hanging white
flowers remind
me of sex,
something to
put my fingers
in. The clover
covering the
lawn like
a population.
Would you
say that
once this
century's
over, there'll
be another
one. I ask
the throng
of barely
bobbing white
heads, soon
to be cut

says Tom.
They're seeding
now. Are they
living. I want
to know. Is
there a spark
of lightning
in their soul.
No, that's
mushrooms
isn't it.
I begin
to believe
in a god
I could
build like
a porch.
I began
to have
a need
like that.
She shall
be fat &
wrap her
arms around
me. She
shall love me
as a boy
& I will
be her
wife. I
ask her
at so many
moments if
this is appropriate.
Anything. Everything.
A blue jay
flings herself
into the open

little tiny
tree. Up &
down, up
& down like
the tree is
that wonderful
three-kinds
of-blue
jay's toy.
If I
shut up
when there's
something to
see. If
I study history
there will
always be
work for
me in
the back
yard. Tons
to gab
about.
And when
I'm not
looking
the century
will come,
then
another
one.

PEANUT BUTTER

I am always hungry
& wanting to have
sex. This is a fact.
If you get right
down to it the new
unprocessed peanut
butter is no damn
good & you should
buy it in a jar as
always in the
largest supermarket
you know. And
I am an enemy
of change, as
you know. All
the things I
embrace as new
are in
fact old things,
re-released: swimming,
the sensation of
being dirty in
body and mind
summer as a
time to do
nothing and make
no money. Prayer
as a last re-
sort. Pleasure
as a means,
and then a
means again
with no ends
in sight. I am
absolutely in opposition
to all kinds of

goals. I have
no desire to know
where this, anything
is getting me.
When the water
boils I get
a cup of tea.
Accidentally I
read all the
works of Proust.
It was summer
I was there
so was he. I
write because
I would like
to be used for
years after
my death. Not
only my body
will be compost
but the thoughts
I left during
my life. During
my life I was
a woman with
hazel eyes. Out
the window
is a crooked
silo. Parts
of your
body I think
of as stripes
which I have
learned to
love along. We
swim naked
in ponds &
I write be-
hind your

back. My thoughts
about you are
not exactly
forbidden, but
exalted because
they are useless,
not intended
to get you
because I have
you & you love
me. It's more
like a playground
where I play
with my reflection
of you until
you come back
and into the
real you I
get to sink
my teeth. With
you I know how
to relax. &
so I work
behind your
back. Which
is lovely.
Nature
is out of control
you tell me &
that's what's so
good about
it. I'm immoderately
in love with you,
knocked out by
all your new
white hair

why shouldn't
something

I have always
known be the
very best there
is. I love
you from my
childhood,
starting back
there when
one day was
just like the
rest, random
growth and
breezes, constant
love, a sand-
wich in the
middle of
day,
a tiny step
in the vastly
conventional
path of
the Sun. I
squint. I
wink. I
take the
ride.

BASIC AUGUST

Summer is endurable
you suggest &
I picked it up off
a wall in Cambridge
today or better
when the chlorine
drips from my
hair down my
back & the
five birds in
New York start to sing.

Brooklyn is just a
ride away. I'm hungry
again! While the ponytail
drips down my back &
I pull on the black
shirt that's wet from
the pool, but so
what, it's August and
the six birds in
New York sing back.

I wish I could
pull a devil mask over
my face. To be in-
visible & assertive,
to scare the hell
out of you. When
you pat my hand
take me all wrong,
make me squirm.
When I feel myself
falling backwards
in my skull

I'd rather race
outside, red &
heavy browed &
scare your thoughts
your pity to
kingdom come.
I'd laugh.

Or I have learned from
novels that you can
stare right through a
person. All the midriffs
of men I have bored
through this summer
in the sweaty subway
which is like
an intestine. I make
the beady eyes vanish
by boring through
like a train
or skipping upstairs.

You have never
wanted anything
I chide myself
as I am walking
through the tunnel.
Does anyone
ever «choose»
life. The ambitious
ones who get
in with both
their sneakers
soaking wet &
their big fangs
wanting all. Privately
I whistle, privately
I'm private. Do we
pound our fists down

like this and go
now, now I must
have for I am
truly here, Mankind!

Is Life perhaps
just another thing
that men own,
like the world
so not having
a greedy antenna
hanging between
my legs I don't
know how to
insert myself
powerfully in
anything's
path. It is
mine tonight,
and shut the
feeling out,
like a light
and in
the dark, get.

I like summer
cause it's
just so hot.
There's no excuse
for such an incessant
daily lack of
relief. The daily
woman with
her breast hanging
out and her
pussy in the
middle of
everything
bundled up

private. For I
must go to
work tonight
and in this
idle unfanned
hour I'll sing
my song. Destiny's
woman at last
in her chair.

If you saw
my heart hanging
out like the
devil face
grinning & pumping
away sweating
blood & grimacing
going ow ow
ow! Kind of
a furless
pussy, my heart

My mother tells
me I am not
her son, my
sister says
that was not my
crime, being foolish
scaring the
mother with
the ugly daughter
mask, hands like
worms reaching
out to the
mother who
has just been
stone so
long that
how could

the mother
bear the
daughter, but
she did
the beautiful
ugly one
of summer
nights. Hungry
like this snake
of a city
reduced to
living stone.

Can you describe
in two syllables
the real
condition of
woman. Like hell!
Would you
strike
your mother
with a stick
call her
bitch, witch
would you
beat her
till she
bled real
water from
her mouth.

The woman
made so many
men afraid,
her incredible
power & smarts.
They froze.
So one guy
said lets tell

her she's
incredibly
ugly, her
power, her
strength
her sexuality,
life coming
right out
of her loins,
lets call
it pussy
lets give
her a hysterectomy
lets tell her
its so uncool
for girls
to be strong
lets tell
her she's
really ugly.

Fear freezes
me daily even
in this heat.
I pay a
bill I feel
better. I live
along. I get
ten bucks in
the mail. Heigh
dee ho. If
I could have
any wish
since I'm happening
since I'm really
seeing here
since I do
& listen. I believe
all the women

could be strong
& stand up &
lock hands
& bond. We
could save
ourselves
we could save everyone
we could be
here tonight
& I am.

.

I've got a
lot of good
ideas but not
one that
will get me
through
August.

OK, I admit
it. I'm a
devil-worshipper.
In a tourist
trap in Salem
Mass my sister
& my lover &
I did
a little dance
on a round
red circle
marked w/
names like
Beelzebub
& Company.

I have
the most interesting
pattern of bouncing
shadow leaves

on my wall
at night. Through
a grid of
shadow window
gate, I
the grown child
wait for
sleep to
overtake me.

In my
devil dance
I began
to look at
the world. On
14th Street
steam pouring
up out of
the street,
steam-pipes
says Sue
that's why
14th Street's
so bad,
bumpy, or
else she
paused while
we looked.
It's the gates
of hell.

Down Christopher
Street where
gayness is going
strong, screaming
drunken but
the pouring of
red-faced
horny souls

down the
street to
the river
where it's also
black & hispanic
& we walk
out on a
Pier, I keep
wondering if
it's okay for
David to be
down here
w/ a woman.
I usually do
this in the day
I explain
remember the
day that
Tim showed
me & Jane
the innards
of the fallen
down pier
building where
everyone stumbled
at dawn looking
for one more
blow job
I suppose.

I been
here, after
I chased
or actually
stumbled after
a girl at
Armageddon,
a club, or
saw you

plunge into
an icy
January hudson
unlike now
inhaling David's
cigarettes
watching Maxwell
house, not
even sighing.
When it's time
to move
we both
know.

You the goddess
of 1988 take me
especial places.
Through burgeoning
Union Square
where I left
my bike &
you criticize
the way I
walk reminisce
about Larry
and you
teach me
about going
slow, each
foot, solid
on the ground
feel it first,
head up, a little
tilted, shoulder
back, clench
your pussy
lift your
butt, let
your shoulders

sway, arms
high. We
should be
in rhythm
it's how
you walk
with a
person. Are
you ruining
me as we
approach our
2nd year
together &
I'm comfortably
in training
to be right
for you
or us, though
I like the
way I
walk alone,
the love
affair
I never
share but
you with
the itsy
bitsy light
of Gramercy
Park it's
great we
still kiss
at corners
in recognition
of trees &
the good
air they
exude. Hot-ter
tomorrow,

a Korean
man assures
his friend.

Friday night
we take
our walk.
The streets
«Dom Perignon
Khaddafy»—you
reminisce
about heroin.
Jean Michel
died this
week. Under
thirty. I
haven't
failed to
be walking
breathing poor,
the fashion
ensemble into
the artichoke
sculpture junk-yard
of Gas-station,
2 Boots is
closed so
we walk to
the hat &
talk about
Zoe who
lives near
here, &
share this
pork with
orange that's
just sensational.
I'm either
in Mexico

or Italy
the unmitigating
heat. Saturday
we stayed
in your
house w/ the
air conditioner
on. I came
out from the
movies on
Friday night
my bicycle
was gone.

By the
time we
got to Cooper
Square we
found two,
one for fifteen
purple w/ footbrakes
you paid,
a thirty-five
dollar one
came fully sprayed
3 gears all
good. Do you
have the
money. Get
them get
them. An argument
began while you
were getting
change, the
guy was drunk
russian, he
was talking
about his
mother which

attracted other
drunks, boys
with tall
beers in
bags. You returned
with a vanilla
coke & we
rode to
the park. A
puerto rican
boy in a
sleeveless
blue shirt was
being lead
away by
the cops
already
in hand-cuffs
his mother
fat in an orange
dress, crying
had to be
pulled away
as they stuffed
him in a squad
car. She didn't
want him to
have a record.
He didn't do
anything everyone
said, he was
so young. He
was so good
looking you
said. He
was. This
is in Tompkins
Square Park.

We saw busloads
of cops at
5th ave, earlier.
Now they were
here. All the
young politicos
in the park
chose to move
then the cops
wedged them
in along
with us on
our new
bikes. Hey.
there were
people with
cards saying
they were
someone
or other. I
always think
the *Village Voice*.
Lots of cameras.
One little cop
who looked like
Benjamin, you
know, the one
who played
Ghandi, said
what's a nice
girl like
you doing
in a place
like this. I
live here. We
both turned
away. I was
separated
from you.

There was a
fat white cop
who was real
sweaty, we
were all sweaty
and he had
a billy club
and he had
this very uncomfortable
«dare me» face
on like a
grammar school
nun. I began
to feel scared.
We dispersed. Pol-
iticos kept
turning on us.
What are you
doing here w/
those bikes. They
live here too!

Out on the street
the cops followed
us out—an
organization of
blue. The street
sang «Go home
Go Home
Go Home!»
The cops were
mad they
wanted to
fight. A skinny
young man
wore a pig
nose & a
Florida cop

uniform. I
think I saw
a girl get
clubbed. I'm
waiting for
the worst
but I
always feel
bored. The
most exciting
violence I
ever saw
was at
high school
dances.

But Basic August
just for now
is a private
demonstration
the writing
on the wall
the teeshirt
says: Free Kelly Michaels.

Kelly's father
comes in and
feels her
breasts. This
is appropriate
behavior in
the families
of devil-
worshippers. There
are leagues
of parents in
America dedicated
to getting the
devil worshippers

out of the
day care centers.
It's obvious.
Either women
should just
stay home
& take care
of the kids
or else the
corporations
should do
the day-care.
They will
give the
kids to
the corporations
early. Give
the kids
to the corporation
not the
devil-worshippers.
The corporation
can stamp
the child
early. On
her wrist
or in her
heart.

Kelly Michaels
made the kids
spread out
in star shapes.
Little naked
white kids
in New
Jersey
worshipping
the devil by

making these
weird patterns
in the music
room upstairs.
Oh she
would drip
menstrual
blood on
the kids &
shit on them.
She made
them clean
it up, the
three or
four year
olds. There is
a very clear
case against
Kelly Michaels
and not
very much in
her defense.
No one came
forward for
her because
you know
everyone would
probably think
that you
were a devil worshipper
too if you
said she was
okay & you'd
never work
in the child
care field
again. I
see lots of
people who

look like
her all the
time in
the street.
I think
she's sending
messages out.
I think
she needs
help. There
were no
character wit-
nesses because
well she
lived with
a girl
and if that
came out
everyone would
know she's
a child molester
because the
two words
lesbian and
child molester
are pretty
synonymous.
This would come
out in
court.

She has
that witchy
little face,
she wears
those
little witch
gloves with
the open
part. She
complained
about

the pay &
poems
were found
On her notebook
cover which
were very
incriminating
which
confirmed
her crimes
she committed
against the
little boys
and girls
who are
now permanently
damaged. They
will see movies
forever of
her big
bloody tampax
dripping on
their faces
during naps.
Who could
forget the
smell of
her
shit.

Let's burn
Kelly
Michaels.
Artsy
creepy
degenerate
probably only
rumored
dyke. Probably
a bisexual.
Too young
to know

better. Very
popular w/
the kids
actually.
They say she
also picked
up a tree
& a car
and played
with a
child's private
parts under-
neath. There
are known
warning signs
if your
child has
been hurt.
Plus they
were given
an anatomical
model, &
if the
kids
play with
the dick
& the
tittie
well something's
amiss. And
no kid
knows
about
a clit.
They have
not yet
been intro-
duced
to its
major
pleasure.

They just
think it's
a piece
of gum.

Kill
that
murderous
bitch
Kelly Michaels
who was
lead
through
the prison
in front
of all
the men
who scanned
her in
silence
a witch
in
shackles.

She might
fly free
one of
these
nights &
her &
I can
talk.
Kelly can
I show
you
my poems.

I know
you didn't
do it.

Maybe you don't
like me. I like
the hairless look.
That's why I
buy tweezers. My
emotions are so
laughable. That's
why I like Tosca.
Spongey blue
earphones get
crammed in
and I bounce
along the asphalt
path watching
the bars of yellow
& blue bounce
in the waters
even east of
FDR. I am
an American.
I am a
true American
poet. I use
multi-strike
cartridges in
my Smith Corona
word processor &
I bash those
words out like
I'm playing
tennis. I bought
so many groceries
today. I deserve
it. The energy
flags & lifts all
night. It comes

on brighter. I
buy Peter Pan
peanut butter so
I can steam
off the
label for my
nephew Nate
who will get
a watch when
he has five.
And I've wanted
this brand all
my life. I
buy drinks at
the bar. One
for me one
for Tim. I
like things though
I don't know
what kind of
thing I am.
All my friends
are coming
and going. I
want to stand
up in America
and say this
is my job,
saying this. Say
I bought enough
things in my
life, or today.
I brought you
a book. You
didn't like it.
I bought a
slice of pizza
it was good.
I bought a

diet coke
My life has
meaning because
I will die some
day. I know
that. I bought
people magazine.
I do not care
how awful
Yoko Ono is
or was. It
should not be
said in print
like that. It
is mean. We
all think we
are the best
& the only one.
That's why I
can't sleep. We
all think we
invented every
thing & then
got shut out.
We all feel
like God dying
on the cross.
Everyday it
is so hot this
summer. I
shudder if
you ask me
if I'm working.
I can hardly
swim. I
can hardly
hold my head
up in the
morning & drink

my first cup.
& then I am
lucky. It
comes over me
an uncontrollable
wave of joy.
I am alive.
I am living
in the life
I used to
come home &
look at at
lunch & wish
that I could
hold. I have
held it so
long it is
moldy. I am
no longer new.
I am old.
Everything is
old. The
planet is
old. & there's
no way to get
rid of all this
plastic. & we're
shooting the
shit into space.
I used to
want to
go into
space. For
what? To
see all this
garbage floating
by. More
than half
the people

on my planet
are slaves
because they
are female.
It's true.
We get
pushed
around. We
don't know how
to fight. Or
if we do we're
called bitches.
Which is an
angry dog.
It's somehow
dirtier than
a dog. A
bitch in heat.
And if you
talk about
it people
say oh are
you a fem-
inist. Which
means are
you whiney &
out of date.
Are you a
loser? Don't
talk about
it. Everything
will be really
okay if you
don't talk
There aren't
as many rich
& famous
women or
female artists

because their
work isn't
good enough
& if you talk
about it your
work is
probably not
good enough
either so
don't talk
about it. It
sounds like
a witch hunt
to me.

It takes one
to know one
Bitch, a
whiney com-
plaining female
artist. Ugh.
Wow. Thank
god I'm
too successful
to talk about
that. I'm
one of the
few women
who are
taken
seriously.

The other
thing that
happens if
you complain
is they
think you're
a lesbian. Who's

that angry
complaining lesbian.
Ever get yelled
at in the
street by
a man—
you, you
lesbian. Ev-
eryone laughs.
Just the
word «Dyke»
is funny.
& you are
a lesbian.
which ruins
everything. No
one can
take it seriously
now. No
one wants
to even hear
about it.
Some people
get off on
it. The
girls are
fooling around
with each
others' pussys
until a man
comes around.
Climax. But
if a man
never comes
around—
what do they
just fool
around with
each other's

pussy
forever. What
do you think
God looks
like. Will
I know when
I die. Will
God know
I'm major
whatever I
am. Can
I trust
in that
love coming
down the
pike getting
larger and
larger till
I come
silently
into
the moment
I'm
standing
in.

VISTA

after David Trinidad

Here I am in
my house. A place
of permanence. Only
dried flowers are
allowed: Goldenrod
from Myra's. Friday's
rain is sizzling. No
wonder I won't
budge. Unpeeling
yellow post-it
pads to reveal
the week's
wisdom: «But this
is just the world.
It's a real gong
show.» A little
stagey but nice.
«You shouldn't
give money to
people you don't
like. On days
when bums
disgust me I
don't give them
a cent.» No
wonder I
stay in. There's
my jeans with the
ass torn out.
An act of
time, not
violence. I lay
old clothes on the
trash cans
out front &

see how many
trips in & out
it takes for
them to vanish.
Once it took
two days for
a shirt to
be gone. To
feel so criticized
by the streets.
My thoughts aren't
staying in. To live
in the streets,
what a thought
what a word.
A doorway could
be a roof, an
abandoned car,
it gets relative
I suppose. For
a few years
people who
know you
take you
in. Feed
you bathe
you, then
even that's
over, if
you live.
I live here
& I write
poems, write
about art
though they
rarely print
it. There's
a hermit in
my soul,

five apples
one with
leaves &
twig on
the wooden
counter. And
beyond the
rusty window
gates there
are trees. Robert
says you could
paint things
your whole life,
the same
things. Cezanne
did. Because
my trees have
gone sparkling
yellow in
the rain
after 11 years
of living
here, it's
a first
to see
the yellow
bouncing
back after
the rain.
I did.
I did
stay here.

It's a new year; you try and stick your keys in
the door. A neighbor's feet are coming down—
your fingers slip. His wrist goes for
the knob—because he's «in.» That's the problem
with doors. The people inside have no patience
with my fumbling. What kind of year is this?
Life is a vow that frightens as it deepens.
You know which ones. I've never written a poem
to you before. Wearing my organs outside.
Or am I in? Lifting myself like a chalice to time.
A can of Coke spinning on the floor.
You're right. I'm different. That might be all
we invented this year. In light of the mass
interpretations, translations, migrations...
In spite of all that it's great that we did
one single thing—to be different.
And now *that it shows*. We should go really slow.
Wearing our difference like streamers or leaves
bringing our gifts to the city. To watch the
monster slowly unwrap us. Naked and forlorn.
And I'm not like anyone else. Feeling my
foot I hear music. Bridging the city.
It's not the poor, it's not the rich, it's us.
And improved public transportation. And cable TV.
I'm giving up the idea of writing a great poem.
I hate this shitty little place. And a dog takes
a bite of the night. We realize the city was
sold in 1978. But we were asleep. We woke

and the victors were all around us, criticizing
our pull-chain lights. And we began to pray.
Oh God, take care of this city. And take care
of me. Cigarettes and coffee were always enough
in my youth. Now when I wake up thousands
of times in the day. I was in the process
of buying my love a shepherd's flute. And a thin
hand picked the one I wanted off the top of the
pile. The one I heard which played so sweet.
And I bought a dud. Hardly better than
a soda bottle. Swell, you said. Well the back-pack
you gave me has started to rip. And the scarf,
well I love the scarf but I keep re-living
that Canal Jean remark. Cause there's no place
for the ironic in plain living. It goes too
fast so you must be direct. Symbolically
I want my black jersey back. Realistically
you must give it to me because I will keep
talking to your machine if you don't.
Our mayor is a murderer, our president
is a killer, Jean Harris is still not
free, which leads me to question the
ethics of our governor who I thought
was good. There is an argument
for poetry being deep but I am not that argument.
There is an argument which chiefly has to do
with judging things which have nothing
to do with money as worthless
because you don't make any money from them.
Did you call your mother a fool when
she gave you your oatmeal in the morning.

I cannot explain my life from the point of
view of all the nooks and crannies
I occupied in my childhood yet
there I sat, smoking. More than anything
I want privacy. If I keep doing this
you will leave me alone. And what about
poor children. Dying in the street
in Calcutta today. Or little swollen
bellies in Africa. A public death
of course has no song. At some point
I decided I would want to die
in my home. And so I would have
to have it, as others would
have to have none. Sometime
after they sold New York
I began seeing you. I was dreaming
but I felt your judgement, and I saw your
face. And a woman stepped out of my
house and she opened the door.

THE REAL DRIVE

PUBLIC TELEVISION

I'm always scared. Aren't
you. In the kitchen
everything is humming,
my mother comments
that what I'm reading
looks heavy. I say
it isn't it's
about television
and go on
to explain
structuralism &
Robert Young
& mention
Zeborah in
passing as
where I
got this
book—
and that's
all my
mother
heard, I
know it.

I don't
know
why you're
not calling
me this
morning.

Is it because
I only wrote
you one love
poem last

August or
is it that
you're ashamed of
me I
fume up the
small winding
hills of Man-
chester, Mass.

There but
for the
grace of
god go
I behind
a woman
my age
dragging
her two
children.

I hurry
home to
remember
which post-card
I forgot
to send.
Can I be
breezy in
a letter?

My mother's
gonna sit
by the
stove. It's
cold in
the kitchen
in New
England.

The sports-casters
are funny
here & the
people eat
a lot and
aren't so
friendly but
they say
hello.

If you
haven't
called me
that does
mean some-
thing. That
I should
mind my
own business
the new
way to
be. There
is of course
a mass media,
the thing
that everyone
sees that
everyone knows
what does
everyone
know, do
they care?
Does it look
okay. Then
there's the
little private
world of
feelings, let's

call that
access.

I don't care
how it
looks, or
if we're
watched by
how many
billion viewers,
see, I am concerned
with having
the important
spot in
your heart
and a channel
to mine
I want
this beam
to be
long and
strong
and true.
Is it?

MY CHILDHOOD

I never got first honors
I got Second Honors.
Mainly I wanted to play
saxophone but they were
so golden & too expensive.
I asked for trumpet (85 bucks)
but he said (Mr. Amarusso,
small head, big body)
I don't think you can play
it with that broken
front tooth...Clarinet!?
No, we've got too many.
And that was that.
Secretly I wanted drums.
At home I had my
bongos & a how-to album
that went dicky docky
dicky docky &
I sentimentally also
sat in the parlor
playing cowboy songs
on my harmonica
and wishing I was
drunk. Occasionally
my mother would
call in from the
kitchen That's
very pretty Eileen.
Naturally I'd flush
and stutter, stop.
What was it about childhood.
I knew I was number one.
The nun said calling me
up to her desk   It's Amazing
Eileen Myles, you have the
highest IQ in the entire

7th grade but from the
faces you make I thought
you were mentally retarded.
You're a pretty girl
you shouldn't screw your
face up like that. There
you're doing it again.
I was doing it again.
I Thundered down
to my desk. Listen
to my feet. I
was the heaviest
girl in the 7th grade.
I always felt gigantic
but they kept putting
me in the middle.
My sister nancy was
born in 1953 and
I had to move from
the small sunny room
on that side of
the house which had
the little private roof
that my father fell off of
many years later, no just 1961.
I had to move into the
larger room with the eaves
that you couldn't do anything
with when I started wanting
to move things, I wanted
to move my sister. My brother
kept almost dying & they
kept re-decorating, pale
blue walls with ships &
men holding small telescopes.
A desk with a golden
machine that changed dates,
a desk blotter. He kept
almost dying and he kept

getting this stuff. It wasn't
all that bad. I had
a dream-boy who I found
on the beach mixed
in with all the seaweed
he was about a foot or
two tall and he was my
friend and would always
stay with me. I only
played with two dolls, Davey
& Timmy. I liked little
Women but my favorite character
was Laurie & I really loved
little Men. I despised
it when Jo grew up
& became maternal. It's just
material, the stone walls around
Jo's school & her old husband
with a beard who sounded
just like her father Mr. March
who was always absent except
when he dropped down a
parcel of copies of Pilgrims.
progress on the hungry girls
Meg Jo Beth & Amy. Why
would Laurie like a bitch like
Amy? There was a Third
Jo's Boys when
they were all old & having
heart attacks, a fat kid
named Stuffy who had been
just re-elected alderman
& died at a banquet. By now
Jo just seemed like the
author. In my childhood
I was allowed to stay
up & watch Mary Martin's
Peter Pan because I was so devoted
to the book. I'd spend endless

hours sitting in my room looking
at the pictures of Peter
in my book imagining other things he
would do, getting all excited. On teevee
Peter was a grown woman with her hair
slicked back talking in a kid's voice, coming
across the stage on wires. I kept looking
at her body knowing she was a woman
feeling robbed & cheated & confused
that they didn't get a real boy to play
the part. Oh I think she's
wonderful my mother said admiringly.
I liked «I've Got A Crow» & «I Won't
Grow Up» but still a real boy would've
been better, more exciting and «I'm Flying»
was stupid because she *was* flying
& also because she wasn't it was
just wires. I couldn't dream at
the peter pan book anymore after
I saw that show but I did
think a lot about flying around
on a stage on wires and whenever
I'd hear Mary Martin's name
I'd feel kind of sick. There
was something weird about her.
There was also a special on teevee
called Aladdin starring Sal Mineo.
It took my mother ages to get my
father to go to bed before it
started so we could just watch it.
He used to talk a lot during shows
we were real serious about wanting to
see. Pointing things out or talking about
stuff whatever we were watching
reminded him of. Eventually crying
because he was no good. This night
it was real quiet right at the beginning
so I was real nervous & excited &
got the rocking chair that night. My

mother had just let the parakeet, Nicky,
out of the cage so she could clean it.
She said Nicky seemed kind of
sick. I was rocking away at the
beginning of the show, when
I felt this lump in the rug. My brother screamed.
Mom. My mother came
in from the kitchen & the bird
was lying just wriggling a little bit
about an inch from the rocker.
Oh my god. My mother said.
You didn't do it she said to me.
Scooping him into the kitchen. She killed
Nicky She killed Nicky my brother
screamed. I didn't even know
he was down there. You didn't
do it, he was sick. You
killed him, you killed him. I tried
to watch the show for a little
while but felt nauseous and went
to bed. Everything felt all ruined from
the inside & I didn't even know how
it happened or what the real truth was.
It was my brother and mother
but it felt like me. Everyone said
in school that the show stunk
& I was a little happier.

ANNE

All things are possible
in my world
I mean really

Aunt Anne put her mother's
clothes on for Halloween
her mother's wig
her dead mother's
glasses.

She never resembled
the woman
but she became
her. It's a
facet of my aunt
which terrifies
my mother
but I find
it powerful
& strangely
beautiful

like looking
death in
the face
and saying
okay,
get going.

THE REAL DRIVE

My great sacrifice exists
between the inarticulate
fingers of a tree sparkling
up through a brooding blue
as I whale it to the gym
in a cab though the air
is wet tonight and I want
to take you in my arms
and go to Europe.

O baby we must. Kissing
all the droplets off your
back in the shower now
and the radiator's sizzling
against the loss and the
apparent despair and decay
in the walls of the way
I live. Anyone can see
it now, even Joan.
I can't change a thing
but it's warm, terrifically
warm against the oncoming
winter of 1986 when I was
born with you who are
always moving your teepee
away, but I usually follow.

I don't want to brow-beat
you, O black and white, black
and white. The cops in the
city whooping down First

like big dogs. I have to
stay true on the street
I was born on, this is
an oath, don't lie.
I am slipping, I am lying.

My great sacrifice exists
because everyone sees it
and I need that a lot.
I am such a big lesbian
that I have to jump
off a cliff. I am such
a handsome poet I have to
become an advocate of
verse and stop lying
and get rich.

Everytime I dress
better pretty soon
I'm speechless or
broke soon I hope.
O release me from
the hostage
of Oh, working for
you baby or what?

In the cab driving
through a slick woman's
arms I could've cried
because I was not
slipping and sliding
alone. It was you

in a beautiful dress
black and white,
black and white
I have felt things here
which I assumed belonged
to fourteen when I
was perfect, oh you
a man or something

wonderful.

The great sacrifice
is—

she slides an icicle
down my blouse
she is a jerk

the wonder of the universe
is   She did not get spoilt

She can hold me
I can hold her
also.

Every bit of ice breaks
up. It flows down the
river streaming.

Tiniest glistening
droplets on the
branches of the
tree this winter

and the dampness
on your hair
in the light

when I go this
way and you
got your

coat, black,
wrapped

around you now
as you walk
home

with the street-lights

on your back

because you
are the
North.

MAL MAISON

And so I got some marigolds
instead of slitting
my wrists tonight.
And guess what I
had to live through
today—hanging on
to the phone with
my desperate wrist
on Sunday, guess
what I had to
live through, what
new shame, humiliation
rejection which I guess
is also worth it, I guess
it is, right, I could be
dead, right—and this
is so much better.
The smell of meat
cooking in the kitchen,
what could be worse,
I know what could
be worse—I could be
pregnant with you!
That's as bad as things
could be. I could be
having you, rather
than having a hamburger.
I could be your mother.
Otherwise I suppose
I could be getting
fucked in the ass &
whipped, going out
to a party or just
eating potato chips.
To count on anyone
is really stupid.

Especially big groups of
them. Glad to be here,
glad to stop you in
your tracks with
their incredible
lack of vision, their
way of continuously
making the future
impossible. I'm
left waking up,
running miles further
than anyone ever had
to before. Thinking
of those bloody stupid
bastards, each one
and their lack of
vision of how great
it could be, I'm not
having you, or having
them or having any
of it. I'm a remarkably
spiritual creature,
I am. Lifting my little
bow & arrow, poignantly
requesting guidance
from the trees or
my feet, or continuous
coffee. It's not con-
tinuous coffee, or
endless. What kind of
coffee is it that
will get me out of
corners, make me move
& keep talking to
people. Look at me
like an arrow on
my bike, whizzing
by like visiting
you. Pouring down

St. Mark's Place,
Quakers, angels
& drunks,
that's all I
see. Lots of
new puppies—
they're in season.

Failure, of course,
is a more interesting
obstacle than
joy. It makes me
stronger, right?
It makes me more
like Winston
Churchill than
the normal
celebrity of
things going
well, procrastinating
& visiting, basking
in my latest vic-
tory about my-
self. What kind
of coffee? Invisible,
bottomless (like Sunday)
and religion. What
kind of coffee?
I'm going running
right now and see
if I can think
of that word.

This enormity
in my chest is
not depression
and I stopped
smoking, started
drooling six

weeks
back, I could
blame everything
on that, even
how close I
am to getting
a puppy, those
kind of feelings.
Mixed with this
intolerable sad-
ness I am learning
to tolerate. I imagine
all the big beautiful
clipper ships sailing
off to sea on a per-
fect blue day and
I am not on them.
You stand on the
dock & wave. That's
what they said to
me as they were
pulling up
the plank.
Yeah, why don't
you try it, wiping
a large sensitive
tear from my eye,
returning to the
town to have
breakfast &
get laid.

Oh, Love, I love
you so much. The crying
babies of the sirens
pass through the
town, I am expected
to do more &
more & more.

I learned
I could leave,
I felt I might
get caught or
else humiliate
myself by
being so
bad, doddering
look at this
autumn acting
like summer,
the world
giving Eileen
a checking
account &
expecting
her to act
up. How
will I know
in this ball
of yarn if
I am acting
or feeling
correctly.

I'm really
depressed.
The best revolutionaries
like to give up on
hot nights in fall
and ponder how
they really
have always
felt like
Joan of Arc
that is
if they
were awake.
And now

I have
a girlfriend
who is really
a cowboy &
now I have
embarrassed
her & really
lost her
again. And now
I am in an orange
dress with this
wild fringe at
a dark party
with big
white lamps
& there she
is! Oh you're
here, you're
here, you're
here. Coming
around the
corner to
where I
work, a large
old church
surrounded
by big iron
fence, a gate
and I'm memorizing
in a movie script
my other life...

OK, I'm this
woman, about
35—she's
been somewhere
else but now
she's here.
In a car, an unimportant

American one, maybe
blue-grey. And she
drives around Michigan,
maybe New Mexico,
Arizona, selling,
God, I don't
know what she
sells but she's
me and I know
all about her
life, how
she sells these
things out of her
car. I don't
really picture
her staying
some place,
her name is Margaret,
I like that. She
may have been
married, had
a kid (or two)
but she left
it for this
dreaming life—
where half-
bored she
roams the plains
of America,
and the painted
desert & the mediocre
cities of Illinois,
etc. She's just
moving her lips
very softly
I am not connected,
I am not connected,
very softly, laughing
very softly occasionally

oh, I am connected
to everything,
winks into the
rear view mirror
at her beautiful
bland sardonic
self, this American
woman, endlessly
riding like
an astronaut
inside the
land, she winks
and pops on
the radio,
hey—what's
that—Sarah
Vaughn singing
Autumn in
New York.
New York, hmmm,
that's funny.
Clicks the radio
off still
smiling, pops
a velamint
into her
mouth. This must
be shot very
close, the
woman's face
is the star,
not her
mind,
her face
is the
star
of that.
The brooding
lips in

America
looking
at the land-
scape
change.
The music
in America,
that junky
scratchy
music on the car
radio, the
endless miles,
all the bad
places to
eat—greasy,
meaty, tons
of men—you'd
think it was
their country,
the baseball
fields, the locker rooms,
war monuments, clubs,
bars, the highways,
the police department,
it's strangely
sinister to
this woman,
and she's wondering
about that.
As she's driving
around this big
sad, fabulous
country. A country's
like a flower
pressed in time,
she laughs
alone. And I'm
in love, all
by myself

for once,
my heart
is a radio,
I just want
to say that
I love you,
and we
have *a lot*
of time. She kisses
another & leaves
again. We are always
leaving, it is
so wrenching
like Autumn
in New York,
my way of loving
you is season
change each
departure
falls through
the air,
it may be
final, frightening
to be part
of something
so immense
the world
going through
a change of heart,
my love for
you, utterly
willing to
be this
woman's face
the wandering
star of the
American mind,
her radio
is in my

heart, I
beg to
be there,
drifting
through
your changes
with you.
Each facial
expression
shifts, the
car wheel
turns as
a leaf
falls
in New York.
I love you,
I love you,
I love you
...I would
never stop

if I was that
woman, but
I am. You
are too,
she's you,
Margaret,
Magda,
woman with the
Letter 'm'
for some
reason.
Perhaps
the Indians
know. Ask
my mother.

Momma, it's
cocktail

hour. The
time is
still
in the teens.
8:18, 8:19
& so forth.
I get separation
anxiety every
time the num-
bers achieve
a new cycle,
the 20s, the
30s. Here
goes the
hour, oops,
there is
another
one coming,
there is,
there is,
there cer-
tainly
is. I'm
drinking
an awful
lot of o-
range
juice, aren't
I? It's very
over-rated.
What is?
Oh...he puffed
smoke thoughtfully
into the horizon
...a lot of
things. Let's
use some
German words
& stuff.

Unterstehen—
be subordinate
to. Another,
gimme another
good German
word. They're
all tough
like that
aren't they?
Untergang.
I am a shipwreck.
I am a hungry
shipwreck.
I like this
German. Let's
keep going.
Fensterflugel.
In the case-
ment I saw
you. It was
the best. You
were framed
(like art)
yet I was looking
down on you.
(Like I like.)
I wonder if I can
go a little further
now. I left
«...and I love
you» on some-
one's machine
today. No response.
I guess she was
just being ac-
cepting. Here is
the finest low-priced
German-English, English-
German dictionary

ever published.
Here on my desk.
Cover design
by Charles Skaggs.
Someone probably
one of you
knows. Charles.
Akzept. acceptance.
Ich habe Akzept. In
German (*auf Deutsch*)
all the nouns are
capitalized which
I think is powerful.
Big strong nouns.
Swift little verbs
pushing the big
nouns around
the language.

NICE WISHES

Mostly I wanted
to wish you
a nice drama,
a piece of tempura,
nice ego trip,
good run in this
ghastly weather.
I meant to visit
you—it looks like
it's going to rain
—How's your leg?
I hope it doesn't
hurt too much.
I wish you a little
corner of my bed
in the morning.
It was charming
how you smiled.
Whenever I see you
at parties I just
giggle or shrug.
It seems that I know
you so much. It seems
there must be something
we can talk about. Isn't
there? We have so much
in common. I like you.
I'm sorry I never wrote.
So that place is downtown,
right? I got the address.
I'll be there. I'm ripped!
I'm so glad you're one

of us now! Now we can talk.
Let's talk. Did I insult
you just now? I meant
it was *nice*. I was being
casual. Sometimes I miss
you so much. I think you
were the only person
I could talk to and
now *I won't, I just won't.*
It just leads to too much.
I know. *I am what I am*
and that's all that I
am. You looked positively
demonic the other morning.
It frightened me, I knew
that look so well and
I wanted to dive right
into your arms also get
the hell away from you
so fast. I wish you weren't
so fucking greedy about me.
It's so sick. I know what
you don't want and that's
what I don't understand.
On the other hand I can't help
responding to you. You are
absolutely like glowing flesh
to me. It's uncanny,
you are so translucent. I
know it just shows all
over my face. You are
the clouds, you are the
sheets. These are nice
feelings. Listen, I like

you a lot. I think it's
great the way you are.
If it's a little dull,
you know it's because
it's ultimately kiddish
to have no deep cross-
current. Compassion
cuts across, friendship
too. Our interest inspires
me, it's so fresh and new
with you. I honestly
understand teaching now.
Like having children,
re-lighting the currents.
The same things are not
The Same. I long for
a teacher. I fear
I am my teacher,
beg for inspiration
on my knees. To several
things. Nice worship
of the human style.
I talk too fast.
You're so brilliant.
You're so weird.
She's like light.
What an ass. You've got to,
I've got to hand it to
her—it's a great ass.
And she discovered him.
Of course. And he hates
her for it. Of course.
Why wouldn't he but so
what. She pointed him towards

his work. She made him
come along. He's so brilliant
now it's accidental. It would
be difficult for him
to blow it now. Look
at him. He's a natural.
He's just so fucking
perverse. That's what I admire
about him. It's what we have
in common actually. My only
fear is I've already blown
it. Poof. Blew it again—
right off my finger-tips.
Treat your fears lightly.
Don't look at yourself.
Look at your friends.
Here, I brought you something.
Sorry I'm late. You can't
imagine where I've
been you big beautiful genius.

DAD'S BAG

Too tired to write about Dad's
bag now. Too late in a big
empty church full of ghosts
& bum choruses outside
on benches going heh-heh,
heh. In a *I Ching* I threw
concerning nourishment,
the corners of the mouth
I was informed I may
have discarded my magic
tortoise, too bad,
it was certainly that
WWII back-pack
I kissed and left
on a trash-can
and vanished instantly
as things well sent
off do, as if they
were wanted elsewhere
or so well used here
they're just gone.
I don't have much to
say about that bag
except that I found
a substitution, a $2
canvas version in
a sporting goods store
going out of business
and I knew I could
be forgiven for
finally chucking
that useless old
back-pack which even
lacked straps by now
and was covered by
black magic markered
globs with blue iridescence

corona-like surrounding
the thick black marks
which covered the horrible
mouths and tongues my
sister had doodled onto
Dad's bag in the early
seventies when Nancy
was practicing being
cool. Ruined the purity
of Dad's bag in my ab-
sense. It was the last
thing of my father's
I owned, maybe a birthday
card he gave me but
that's different. Let
the man die, right.
He's 23 years gone now,
I knew him less than
I've remembered him
by now, I never even
knew him. I knew his
name, I realize he was
in a war and liked
to sing and just this
last June I was sitting
somewhere in California
and I started crying
because I realized
how really sad I felt
when he died, and I
think he actually
loved me and I think I felt
very abandoned when I was
eleven and didn't know
what to do about it ex-
cept wear grey clothes
and start pissing my
pants when I laughed.
Odd reaction. My deepest
fear was that people

would think I was insane.
Was going to lose control
laughing too hard. Listen
Dad, you just got to under-
stand I can't be carrying
this thing around any-
more. I can't be fixing
it—I brought it to the
cobbler's and the dry-
cleaners and no one
knows how to put straps
on a rag, and where
would I wear it anyhow
and I can't hide it
anyplace in my apartment,
it's just an old piece
of faded cloth with
rusty clips and a
nice button & I looked
at the number a thousand
times and couldn't find
any significance, it
was not an important
number. So, knowing
that it's not you
at all, it's this
old bag, Dad, it's nothing
else and, well, you know
the rest. Some old shit-
bum has it tucked under
his scalp in a door-way
right around here, may-
be he died, maybe it's
been owned by two dead
men by now. I only
know it's late and
I'm tired and it's
off my hands.

NOVEMBER

Because I'm sure that nothing lasts
I have to be very sure where I am
I can hear the dripping of the faucet
and the cries of little birds outside
and I have to be very sure that I love
because I'll never live like this again
and I'm sure that I love

I'm sure I'm closing in on something
the building isn't making that angle
of light for me. But I can see it.
It silences the cat but it doesn't silence
me. That's why I let the cat be
around. My landlord doesn't think
my way. I couldn't be like that.
I'm sure that I love.

Obviously my heart lies clenched
in my fists. I must be thinking or
feeling this way. This poem's bad.
It wants to think or tell about
how it's felt. But it just seems
to beat along between punches
and silence.

I have to be very sure where I am.
I'm telling you so. If it weren't
for telling I'd be left with the plumbing
and birds, where I am, but I'm telling
you so.

I thoroughly respect the birds
because they're not even listening.
I do. I like them a lot.
For their poverty and lack of thought.
I love myself for my love, a dubious

gift, and I guess I need those
fucking pipes. Simplicity,
that's that. I guess I love you
and I need you, love telling you that
I have to be very sure where I am.

Listening and waiting.
I wish you'd call and tell
me something, my landlord wants
to know where I'm at, but
I'm telling you that nothing
lasts, it doesn't silence me
but it silences the cat
I have to be very sure where I am.

CATHLEEN

I was listening to the Santa Claus
Samba and I was thinking well
she wound up in the street
anyhow and I thought
well at least she influenced
me to buy new jeans

I was stooping like her at the reading
and who was it she claimed
to know. She said I wasn't
punk at all. I was living
here since the rent
was cheap. You call that a phone?
No shit Cathleen. You broke three
lights and really stunk. Two
year old jeans that were
torn at the knee. Everyone
knew who you were, Cathleen.
And I was amazed by
your scars.

HIM AND OTHERS

Etienne de Silhouette, remember him?
How about Silenus? I think I'm
bound to be forgotten
by you and others just
like you—you and yours.
It's amazing how it all whisks
past. Really, what could've
been, blithe memories, cigarettes
the fastest planets have no
time for things that cling.
Thoughts. Silly. I'd rather
sink my teeth in your neck,
seriously, knock you down
on the floor—all for love.
You'll forget my lousy
poems but if I could just
mar you or something. Nothing
nice ever sticks but boy
a scar—if I could ever
really bruise you with
my feelings, them, so infinitely
forgettable & gone.

I don't know no one
anymore who's
up all night.
Wouldn't it be fun
to hear someone
really tired
come walking
up your stairs
and knock on your door.
Come here
and share the rain
with me. You.
Isn't it wonderful to hear
the universe
shudder. How old it all,
everything,
must be.

How slow it goes, steaming
coffee, marvelous morning,
the tiniest hairs
on the trees' arms
coming visible.

I like it better,
no one knows

sweetness, moving your
lips in silence.
Closing your eyes all night.

It's so much better
disarming myself
from terror, and light
passing through
a painting I stuck

on a window
earlier, when I was scared.

It's great, it's really great.
Trees hold the world
and the weather
moves slow.

Even a body dissolves
and takes a place, incorrectly,
everywhere I would
like to nuzzle,
and plants a heart
in the world
voiceless.

I began knocking.
Ridiculous. Just to hear
your echo back,
arm against face

just to stop those fucking
trucks, my thoughts
of vanishing
into that sweetness.

SPINNIN WHEEL

For courage or calm
I drink this balm
old song in
new form. I walk across
your room, arms
down—remember warm
stretched out.
Don't. That's all I do.
But don't. Rock, rock,
rock. Okay,
but I came back.
Again, again
not over, Little Dark Tide,
Oh no, not you,
not you so after
all again. You,
my curl, protection.
Oh no—the blanket
splays open
it's cold
n slow...

I have the same
birthday as John
Milton. Did
you know that?
So I don't have to
write long poems about
heaven & hell—everything's
been lost in my lifetime
& I'm usually blind drunk
and not so serious
either. However...
when I am nearly dead
will you read to me
in bed? Will you pre-
tend to be my daughter
or my wife, whoever,
will you crawl in
& die with Me?

A good enough reason for leaving
well enough alone. Feeling. My mother
dragged us to those cemeteries and cried
because she loved the guy and we stirred
on the grass and felt uncomfortable
and sometimes kneeled. When my
father delivered mail he was also tired,
exhausted and depressed. My mother
was alone all day with us until he started
cracking up cars so she got a job and
till he died she worked. She kept
working when he died but we owned the
house so it was sort of frivolity.
She told stories about work almost
in the same way my dad used to
do only we had to respond. Daddy
did it for impact. Right away I
started baby-sitting. I would buy
my own clothes if I couldn't have a paper
route and a good bike. I had to figure
out what my habits were—buying
singles, buying mom flowers in the sub-
way. I wanted to make my brother
& sister feel like shit. They didn't
miss him or feel that glad that he
was gone. We couldn't talk to each
other about this. He was such
a goof, and such a demanding and
pathetic guy, my father, her husband.

NEW ENGLAND WIND

Remember me this summer
under the eaves again
stretched out against
the sky again
like Orion's moon

when a breeze crawls
down a screen, pip, zing
or is that a cat
crawling up

Oh was I alone in the
first room I ever
had or who would've
writ this then? Me too
when I am mad.

O leave me alone with
my aching head,
panicky panicky
no where to go
pretty north & silly

the other night
under the eaves
in a rain at 4 o'clock
I woke up it was
so sexy; listened so
careful in the world
the next day
for who also heard it
dreamy-eyed, who could've
come up or I come down
for once from
the sky
to be what
fell.

No, it's not about greatness
or being human—lucky or
unlucky enough to
hear bombs falling
outside your window on
the Fourth of July, 1983.
Some people have stayed
up, some voices are out there
talking, jawing through
the night and across
the stars I'd like
to connect a couple
of humans and I do
so silently I introduce
them like children
do—they assume
that all the humans
they've ever cared
about should meet
and will somewhere
in time and the
summation of all
those meetings
somewhere tell us
that we have a function
just to be alive and
hope. The tone that
they call elegiac
doesn't do justice
to anything at all
and I am even
beginning to resent
the light accompanying
me since the world
seems a little thin
or smooth without you. It's

alright to pick
up the phone
and it's pretty late
like someone sleeping
whole needs to
know what's missing.
The details escape
me. Someone who
knows wants to know
more and they
couldn't know enough
I couldn't tell
them that the night
is so elegant
and life seems so
much deeper
just for a moment
in your vanishment
you almost exposed
its secret.

PONDER

All the blankets are
mine this time
even the sounds
which the
blankets are made up
of—those birds
are singing this morning
of thee, me
& you can have it
but I happen
to be here
somehow. Adulthood
Yuck is so first
hand. I come
from a hockey
town, it's where
I was born
the amount
of water
I was born
near, but nothing
about me.
Everyone was
just skating.

The poet must steal some
fire he said
& then he will steal
it from her.
I closed the
book. It wasn't
what I had
in mind.

A network of branches
could be just like
a brain, I guess
they just are
he slept here
once & I told him
about her
I'm just like Jesus
this is my little
myth
so I told him
& he got really
cold so I guess
he died. It's all
as embarrassing
as wanting
a puppy, or a
child hanging off your breast
I like bad days better
than good
if there was something
to steal I probably
would be the
first one to
go out

you'd think we all were
these fucking messages
listen to the cars
we're all at the party
can you hear me,
can you hear me
excuse me I just
wanted to get desperate
for a sec

the fellow with the baby
my friend Bob
compared the situation
I've been pondering
all of this since
yesterday, you see
I'm currently
looking for work
& you know, Sex

he said something
was like losing your
virginity which
men think about
I just thought
about getting knocked up
but no I'm not sure
I feel it ever happened
to me, I mean I sound
like I'm wondering if
I ever lived, Doubt,
I don't know if
I ever even had the stuff
I hate to think
I ever functioned
as a lane
for someone else's
desire, now let
me think, who did I lose it
to? Some girls just
wanted to get rid
of it. Oh I'm a diamond
in the rough but
you can't see me.
I lost it once in August
& then again in

January, all the divisions
are lost. There was
a party at a bar
and when it was over
you couldn't tell
it just turned back
into a bar. This
is the point (Maybe
I'm raping you, huh?—
Should you wake up
a sleeping woman
to tell her someone
else just died
were you anxious, or
just jealous, I mean
was that like
getting fucked?

MAD PEPPER

I wonder if anything really needs to be revived.
MAD magazine should probably be dead by 1984
rather than: $2.50 CHEAP. It's difficult
to impossible to just buy pepper. You
can get a vast amount on sale for $2.99
an exquisite amount for $1.49—nicely packaged
like a spice but it's just pepper. The tall
waiter leans over and says: Would you like
some freshly ground pepper on your salad?
Oh yes. Leaning over to my companion—
Oh, this is nice. Dan recommends I go
to MeadowSweet and get some special Lesbian
Pepper. Pepper's male I snort. I want
some cheap male pepper. *The Village Voice*
made me miserable, that damp scuzzy paper
those endless articles I should really
read and when I do I know less, wasted
a night or a morning. I boldly returned
and exchanged the *Voice* for *MAD'84*,
at least it's a pleasure owning that
silly gloss and will be entertained
at least once thinking: MAD's not the same
as it used to be. Tennis anyone? The
margin was the best. Why don't women
have back-room bars. It just wouldn't
work, that's why. Pepper's male,
sea salt's female, it takes longer
to gather, waiting for the ocean
to dry up and come back, overwhelmed by
the immensity of it. It's nice to have

a friend like you to sit on the shore
with. Maybe I'll bring some pepper.
From MeadowSweet. I seek adventure
today. Wound up in a hardware
store, a meeting, superette &
a bodega looking for pepper. First
today I craved cheese, then (now) I crave
fish, some sushi to go, it's cheaper,
quick, broke again but I got my tools:
Spackle pan roller, Scotch-brite pads
Ajax, all strong names, I look strong,
I must be strong. I bought Lotto,
I left early thinking I would meet
the thing in the street, I met Leonard
bumped into Tom in a coffee shop, that
was the thought, got confused in a
hardware store, the help looked junked
out, I had to pee, walked back to
the coffee shop, asked for the
key, but the door was open. Oh, yes,
I got my hair cut today on Astor
Place, near the mall, where the pathetic
belongings of all are sold. Again &
again. Poverty's an ocean. I bought
a pen, a red one, reddish orange.
What do you think of the Lower East Side
Art Scene. Oh I don't know I guess
it's great. I mean I'm not connected,
I just bumped into a guy I know is
successful. He says he's trying to
not let it affect him, but still
I wondered if I said the right thing.
I think it's nice the neighborhood

looks different so I don't have to
move and my apartment's worth more.
So now I have to paint it because
the face is depressing, the face
of poverty. You said it's female
didn't you? That the face of poverty
is female which is a good line, it sounds
like a good line, but it takes more than
sound to make a good line. If you could
put real truth in a line it would never
be a good line. That's a good line.
It sounds true, doesn't it. A good
line sounds true.

Pepper's male is a good line.
But that's because it sounds
more like a place, Pepper's Mall.
I live in Pepper's Mall, New Jersey,
it distorts. It looks like it's going to rain.
Big things probably sound small at first.
Someone asks you for something and it
sounds really unimportant: Give me some
poems, I'd like to translate them into
Serbo-Croatian. Sure. Hound me, Bitch.
Later you get a post-card from Beograd
& you realize she wasn't kidding.
There could be a statue of me in the City Square
by now. Next time someone says pass me the
pepper, give it to them fast. I'm shy about
asking for things. I could sit at the table
dying but I can't get the necessary eye con-
tact from over there to ask for the butter.
I start saying, well you don't really need

it. That's right, pushing my beans around
merrily passing everything even my fork
to anyone who looks up in a flash. The strongest
things I know...humidity, fire-crackers, hunger,
the capacity of trees to grow leaves, it's what I
see when I'm looking around, I miss you so
much, but you are not the strongest thing
right now but what I see. Against a brick wall
a woman with one of the most beautiful bodies
I have ever seen drapes herself against three
dark sisters who carry her apparently in
something called *Bewegungsstudie*. Motion Study
my dictionary *ubersetz*. I won't even tell you
what I thought, Pepperhead. Thursday, August
2nd. Some part of me is always quietly counting.
I think that is a good line. Stooges Anonymous.
Beverly Ipswich Rockport. A train schedule
I carried when I got on the wrong train.

The red light continues to blink on my answering
machine and I stepped out ages ago to pick
up a coke and some pepper, some cigarettes
Handy-wipes, I love them, and everything changed
it will never come back that clear single in-
tention, though it seems there were two or three.

I could get a poem
out of sailing down
the Hudson on a piece
of shit. Did I ever
tell you about the
night I went into
the kitchen area
to get more valium
I couldn't sleep
& swallowing more
fell down & hit my
head on a pipe
and was so mad
I could have
cried that he was passed-out
on the couch & if he wasn't
there to hear me fall
down on the floor
what was he there
for? Hiding from his wife?
Endless poetry days, cruising
around, airing out people
from their house
letting each one
buy me a beer
so I could quickly
explain my desperation
& take you on
to the reading and the party
and then to my house to
feed you valium so we
wouldn't have to fuck.
I get drunk with men
in my sadness
I miss my daddy
my mother does not understand

me (I love her!)
I'm too heavy for the average
lesbian. I'm really heavy!
Someone a little straight
like her can understand
a little drunk
gross with men
dirty around the
edges, horny
understand that my speed
is my attitude
I'm really all flowers
inside and you can
really have them
I'll name them
for you.
This is coffee in the morning
waiting for the day to pick
up. My life is like
a tray of ice-cubes
your face smiling
on each little
block until they
melted and I
was all alone
on the couch pulling
my hair out,
never going out.
All alone. Shadows
surrounded me.
This is my life, the Underworld?
Nope, little torch came back
& burned it all down.
She did. She picked it up
and turned it over
like a big cake.
& I had such hope.
Bullshit. I was 33 and wanted
a Wife. Couldn't it be

someone like you
that I knew?
Damn. Fuck. Piss. Shit.
The months of wailing
and bright cheeks.
Hi Eileen! How are you?
Great, I roared.
The bottom marched on.
Now a year has passed
& I read these things.
A life as simple
as a coloring book
being crayoned
in by who knows
what. You bitch.
You page-turner,
You Fool!

KEATS & I

Keats had
his luxuries
& so do I.
Damned if
I know
what they
are. All
this everything,
the day
when the
rain stops,
my vision
is excellent
what I
lost is
what I
know the
emptiness
creating a
whole which
excellent
winds come
through
like I
am a lamp.
Here let
me extend
my arm
to you like
a tree. A
willow pouts
up in the
Lower East
side, you
know this
whole area

used to
be a swamp.
Still is &
we laugh.
I love my
excellent
luxuries but
I don't know
what they
are. Don't
stop me.
I didn't
know I
wanted to
go on.
Sampling
these airs
which you
play. I
accept evolution
easier than
a remedy,
Keats bumped
his down
in cavalier
fashion, liked
it cool yet
some cayenne
for his tongue.
I bought
these black
dungarees
which aren't
my favorite
the day when
my crotch
gave out
at Jackie's
now that

sounds lewd.
It was
a rainy
day like

this and
oh the story
is silly
to tell—I
have others.
I replaced
old pants
with another
pair— «we
call them
pant»—
I bought
a pant
downstairs
the language
surely
lost a leg
I'm getting
silly like
I'm shaking
the last
drops of
rain from
my head.
A space was
created today
in the city,
and a thunder
was heard
on my machine
I recorded
it by accident
when I was
searching for
a word, the

weather broke
Boom which
was my message
I believe. You'll
get it now,
I let it in
as she slipped
quietly out of
town over the
weekend—
So what! Absolutely
nothing matters
in the way
that I feel
the most emotional
space—Oh
Silly Me, Oh
Silly Silly
twinkling my
toes lifting
a smoke to
my lips,
the window
full of buildings
& trees, the
swoosh swoosh
of traffic
on the wet
black street
which was the
song you were
playing for
me the first
one happy
& so pretty or
the one you're
playing now,
uncontrollably
sad, oh now

this one, of
course, now
you're stopped
& I can hear
the people
talking in the
street, children
squealing, a more
ambitious motor
chugs up & passes
& now again
you're playing
a lighter sweeter
song. And I
notice the
rain has
begun. What
time is it
now, 7:03?
Will we be
forever waiting?
My problem,
my disease
the soft
rain in the
trees on Avenue
A, a church
with a little
green tower
that holds
a bell I
never heard
I don't hear
it now—
I feel its
presence, I
suspect it.
Try to tell
a flashlight

about the
dark things
in the room
try and describe
I can only
describe the
reality of children
from the reality
of being a child,
once, and you
might imagine
this limited but
you have never
had this feeling
or you did
& then it
stopped. I started
thinking about it
& it started again
I often feel
trapped in
insouciance,
keeping my
balance in
a song that
is either
too short
or too long.
I throw
all kinds
of seltzers
& teas down
in a cavalier
fashion—it
seems I was
born thirsty
& that is
unhealthy. It
bloats the

organs &
all that
revolting shit,
once when
uptown running
around the
trail in
Central Park
& stretching
afterwards
I commented
that at times
I thought
of my insides
as filled with
smoke & fluids
all charged up
at other times
packed like
a pig, stuffed
with organs, &
tubes thorough-
fares, the way
it is. My
friend said
she like the
sound of
the first better
I did too
but it's really
both isn't it,
an awful
lot going on
that's what
I'm doing
right now
as you're
playing such
energetic

then thoughtful
strains. So
much work, it's
actually thrilling
I almost said
«almost» but it's
actually better.
I believe in
a community of
believers. It's
the most believing
I do which
creates faith,
important to
me & Martin
Luther. What
constitutes Poetry.
A Lapse? Into
everything?
I have no
doubts it's true.

Let's drink buckets
of coffee. Let's
imagine ourselves
all fired up
for once. I
mourn (frankly)
what's left
my space, I've
got no substitute
for myself or
anyone else,
doppel-ganger
is my favorite
joke.
I leave comic
messages on
my machine,

I go natural
I get strict,
whichever way
I go it's alright
a loose tooth
I need a
remedy
for my mouth
a gaping hole,
I feel like
an animal
tonight, earlier
when I
heard a person
moved to
another city
last weekend
when I was
oddly feeling
your presence,
expectant &
I'm mourning
it by the
windows & the
trail of flats
& sharps that
occupy the
back part of
my brain
its stem
the ancient
part, the
book I read
in morsels
late at night
the time I
reserve for
reading—
if I read

In the morning
especially
about the
brain
I'd never
start. Simply—
if you read
about the
foot you'd
never be
walking at
all. If you
drink Irish
Breakfast tea
at night or
at twilight
would you be
violating someone
somewhere, any-
where at all?
I ask these
questions fervently
I write through
cocktail hour
the cardboard
cups are in
their plastic
bag in their
tin bowl
on the window
still full of
air & I
feel a hunger
coming in
those piggish
insides. I come
around with
appetite to
parties, see

appetite in
people's eyes
asking me questions
I answer
back & I
dance. I
take the
appetite home
to its bed
and read
about the
brain. It's
an odd life
and the
music has
stopped. There.
Jingling, starting
growing. I'm
hungry. I
kill his mineral
water. I *see*
a prism in
the glass. I
write words
I didn't think
—*send* for *see*
etc. The *bee*
boo of the
siren blocks
the music. There
now that's
the phone,
thronging.

My matchbook
says: AREA.
I word to
meet rather
than space.

I feel
this area, your
departure, this
loss has
created an
excited, sad
cerebral hungry
area I constantly
allow to swim
along, what's
this some
Wine Vinegar
bobbing to the
surface of
the AREA above
his refrigerator.
His area seems
to attend a
family, various
accoutrements
empty

I hear a
gate close
rattle, rattle

it's quarter
of eight, «Let
me play
one tiny little
short one
it's always,
it's my «ender.»
And he does
it tinkle
tinkle   chang
chang   trill
churl, that
word, we get

no new
ones   peep
loop   dong
dong, hopeful
full, tworl,
dun dun dun
deep—reel,
cheep, dun,
dun, I wish
so, so, fervently
to be together
going out
working
into wet shoes.

I love the guy in the laundromat
the way he hands things to me,
smiling, a nice pink slip
with a black number on
it. I've just handed
all my clothes over
to him, they're quickly
weighed, priced, he writes
the price down on the
slip and it's okay,
he smiles, I smile,
I walk out. It's funny
how I sit in this, the
inner sanctum of my
apartment with
the stove, the refrigerator,
overhead light. Down
there in the dark by
the window I've
got a desk but I like
it over here—it seems
warmer though the
radiator's down
there—I live
in a small place
and when I'm alone
I make it smaller
prefer it this
way, keep the action
in a small bright
place, wonder
where I'm going
but tonight
I've got
this light.

THE SUNSET CHORUS

Ambition is sturdy, isn't
it? Like being able to
bear the cold or
allow the heat
or anyhow it is windy
today and walking
helps me drive
the sleep into
my hair or someplace
where it doesn't
matter. Lounging
in your office
made me aware
of the necessity
of work in people's
lives. By five
it's peaking
in your office
excited voices
all about their
jobs, exciting
stuff, I'm not sarcastic
they like it & I wish
I had a place to
do it too, freshly
painted, great
machines, a whole
art department
delivering up
the new ideas.
Shampoos, horny
romance novels
for the subway
ride and lunch
at your desk. It's
food for the imagination

and soap for your
head so you won't
be funky when
he lays you down.
I run down by avenue
C & D in dirty
golden sweats
& they're selling
the works, « 1984, »
cop stops a New Jersey
car who just copped
& I saw his face
go white: I'm ruined
my job, or somebody
just won't take
this one more
time, she'll
leave me. Alongside
the 2nd Avenue
entrance there's
more men & women
than ever saying:
just some money
for food. Just
a quarter to get
on the train.
Some nights it's
raining & it
breaks your
heart as you're
rushing home
to this, what
looks like
a dump, cheap
food—I can
smell it from
here, tofu
in the pot.
There's a sunset

on my file
cabinet, red, purple
skies, orange gold
clouds, a volcano

white and grey
coming up to
meet them
the heavenly
stuff. The same
argument is pursued
inside everyone's
hearts and veins
whether you
name it or
not it's
really the
same, even
if you only
step out
of your car
for a moment
you can't
help feeling
the day, wondering
how much
really needs
to be done.
How can
you possibly
accept
it?

TRIANGLES OF POWER

Got a slice
burned the roof
of my mouth.
Knew I would
it was
delicious.

I fast-walked
someplace. My feet
were cold
but the
slice built
a fire
in my
stomach.
I said
Thank you
to the
natural
elements:
cold night
digestion.

What is
it about
the January
feeling—
past everything
else, low-glowing
hunger that
propels me
around
I may be wrong,
predictable
to picture you
around here

or us over
there, it's a
miracle,
rolling golden
in the coldest
month looking
forward &
back from
so much
else, there
wasn't even
a noun around
I walked
in from
the snow
nearing Christmas
& you touched
my black
coat
with your
handsome
hand &
believe me
I came
lit. (&
am changed.)

THE BICYCLE

My bicycle, this ugly machine
sits in my apartment. It stands,
leaning on its little red
stick just like a funny
person with a bell on
its shoulder. My bike,
she's a girl. Smoothly we
travel the streets at night
we get home fast
I lug her up. Two flights,
roll her in, *There.* It's
not my habit to be so instrumental,
so musical...I used to leave her
downstairs. I never left her
outside overnight—I wouldn't
do that. But what does she
mean? Down on the elevator
praying she's outside
waiting for me...*She is!*
It's the first night & she
met the other friend,
my apartment. It looks good.
They get along. May the lights
in my home speak well of the
new pair, Movement and Stillness.
I set off a gallant light
to encourage a gong.
My bike and my home
get along.

It's something like returning to
sanity but returning
to something I have
never known like
a passionate leaf
turning green.
August almost gone
«—That's my name,
don't wear it out.»
As if I doffed
my hat & found
a head or
had an idea
that was
always mine
but just came
home, the balloons
are going by so
fast, I lean on
buttons accidentally
jam the works
of what works
when I simply
am this
green.

A POEM IN TWO HOMES

Everywhere I go
is home

when I'm dreaming.
Creamy traffic

pouring past
the Noho Star

‹I thought you were
coming to my
home!›

I am.
Okay.

At my back:
all of Bleeker St.
the confusing

part of New
York life

three generations
back. Today:

fruit stand, bad
bars: Stormin'

Norman & Susie,
old cafes, Village

Oldees, depression
now, the Bleeker

Cinema—Some
interesting ‹film›

Become a member
of the Bleecker
St. Cinema

your first year
in town. It's

doubtful I will
move to Atlanta

for business. To
Texas to teach.

Remember Soho. This
is Soho. There's
just these two
bars and then

the OG where
conceptual artists
sat all day

you can hardly
hear it, my
poetry. It's

in danger of
vanishing if
I don't write

it down. Does
it change like
the neighbor-

hoods, yes,
if you don't

buy it in a flash
well who knows

what'll happen
to you? You'll
wind up in the

lower east side,
one day all cobble-
stoned with

trolley tracks &
dairy restaurants
like some old

world. There was
a giant line out-
side that old

church on New
Year's day. You

couldn't get in
so you went &

had coffee
with the

guy who depressed
you, Noel Sack.

Eileen, why don't
you work he
said.

Noel, I sd
waving my hands.
I bought his

old speakers
& my check
bounced.

That was the
last straw.
He was so

pissed. I
guess he's

in California
or someplace.

We went to that
history of the Avant
Garde Cinema

at the Modern Art.
I didn't want
to be

with him at
all. His teacher
Duncan McNaughton

writes me about
the ‹real thing›

poetry that's not
what, language,

ethnic, lesbian
black, you
know like Charles
Olson.

I packed all
of my clothes
from your

home into a
Macy's shopping

bag. Oh gimme
that jacket, I
wanted to

wear that. And
walking up twelfth
brrr it's

really cold. Gimme
that white tur-
tle neck.

I did not forget
the yellow legal
paper folded

with the stripes
going up. I
forgot the tan

notebook full
of numbers
I've got
to call. I'm
walking home

with a Macy's
bag and one sweater
& a head band

in it. Her soul
is not a great
soul. She dwells

on domestic things:
her love. Her walk
in the cold &

even keeping to the
tiniest rule makes
me full.

My home becomes
a prayer mount
when I get

there—full of
light & dust &
the answering

machine blinking.
Hello Eileen, I am
Joel Lewis. I

am the world's
greatest poet.

I do not seem
to be obedient
to the world

today. Since
television, there
has been

me. It has
been a tall
order to carry

out, the whole
case for enter-
taining literacy

on *my* back.
i was listening

to a tape of
Patti Smith yes-
terday in

my home. It was
before she had
a band & everything

in her voice
was waiting
for it.

And, even better,
oh dear god,
andro-

gynous creep
in the sky,
Danny heard

Hitler & he
says Hitler
so bumble

bumble, not much
blurrr facts,
bull-shit

& then he exploded
you didn't
know when

& that was
what moved

the crowd. The
freedom of
exploding

in the air
Hitler, Hitler,
Hitler pop
Hitler

I want to
be Will
Rogers

that's what
I want to
be. And,

that folks
(twirl twirl)
is the

end of the
world. As
we know.

I think I will
be the anti-
christ. Rather

than simple
Eileen Myles.

Poor she. The
anti-christ
is me. I

died at the
age of 33
yet I

walk the
streets of
the east

village joyful,
and remorseless

like a cruel
& perfect

poem, my
butt, unsold.

Sometimes
I act vague

about my
lesbianity

No, it is
deeper
than all

I know. The
softness, the
flagrant

disposition. To-
day I used
half a jar

of Dippity
Do & I
got it right.

I will lay
my plastic

head on
your shoulder
& weep.

For you, but
not for
me. My

compassion is
boundless &

incredible.

My mission is
not so predictable
as reverse

of the first.

I take some
of this
& some of
that, I
wiggle

unlike Christ.

I'm not a
girl, nor
a boy. I

won't bear
child.

nor knock
you up. I
do not

come w/instructions
even to myself.
All my notions
are felt

i think, as the
arrow
strikes the

fatty part
of the

arm of
the boy martyr
I am unwounded

wet from the
well. I am
clear-eyed &

burning with
dispassion

like Christ,
but different.

Zounds
love that word.
Zounds. It

resembles arrows.

Each panel

represents a dif-
ferent industry
or else each
panel represents
a different re-
ligion or masonic
lodge, or else
each panel re-
presents an age,
like the awful
age of pisces
which we're
leaving as
we're chugging
on towards
the great
new mysterious
age of Aquarius.

Everything you
can think of
that seems
mysterious
everything's
going
to be
like that.

A sphinx would
make you

happy because
at least
a sphinx
is a fact.

We're coming
from there,
the desert &
we're going
right back
in. Now

more than
any other
time in
history, you
really ought
to please
yourself
because
in mysterious
winds a
cave inside
your soul
might be
the only
place
to go.

So why house
a skunk?

Once my whole
apartment is
grey I can
think this
all out.

But I'm
hardly
ever home. Hi,
I barge in,
all smiles,

machine is
blinking away
& my hands
all full of
direct mail
envelopes. Salvation
Army. gay direct
mail, poor Bowery
guys. culture.

Everybody wants
money. And
I just came
home from
a hard
day of looking
for money
for my
organization,
that of
the poet

In your
decline
I sing
your song.

At the end
of the
world
I am
my poem.

HOW I WROTE CERTAIN OF MY POEMS

In the summer the city seems like a big rotten museum, or an empty abandoned culture where no one lives anymore which suits me just fine. For me the holiday weekends in the summer are the kind of wreck for which I feel like the ideal narrator—so being in the city for the 4th of July weekend was kind of a set up for this poem. The city's outsides look like your insides if you're feeling that way. I was. My «love» life was a mess. Someone old was around and so was someone new, and I felt that was also immediately bound to be old. She had no place for me. I could see it. I didn't even know if she was in the city or not that weekend. I told Alice Notley about my situation and she said it sounds like you're getting ready for a major work.

Ten years ago I wrote a poem called «Romantic Pain.» At the time I was doing a lot of speed, I was in love & was writing a pamphlet for Franklin Library about the life of Hart Crane. Michael Lally was the editor & he was giving these great maddening jobs to all the poets. I read a biography of Crane (Voyager), his letters and his poems. I became him. I wandered around Manhattan that year in flowing coats, being mournfully Crane. I was 27. I rode the Staten Island Ferry one night & it spawned that poem for me.

I repeated that trip last summer, emulating myself at last. I made New York into Disneyland on the Fourth of July weekend, taking all the rides of my life. I live on 3rd St. and I attended the Hell's Angels block party. I felt like my life had been turned into an amusement park. It was awful. My favorite film-maker is Fellini. I wasn't necessarily ready to kill myself but everything I looked at made me think about death. Crane's line, «My Dear, I've simply disgraced myself» was uttered to Peggy Cowley just before he neatly placed his raincoat on the boat rail & hopped over it somewhere between New York and Cuba never to be seen again.

I tried to get an agent of late. She told me they were really into fiction these days, that's the market. You kind of write like a journalist, like maybe...I hope you don't consider this an insult, maybe Jill Johnston. I love Jill Johnston—that's no insult. I don't get this fiction thing, though. I really don't. They want their rides polished, is that it? I'm starting to write plays now so I can see invention from that point of view. But I don't make up much, she's probably right. I don't think most poets do. Even Blake was really there.

There's a line in this poem (Hot Night) I'd like to explain. «...I can't / because it is not beautiful / & I'm a ward of the / state.» I meant the state of beauty. I'm a ward of the state of beauty. Even as it rots & corrupts (Love) I still have to watch. I shot a roll of film that weekend. I was with a friend, Katie Cooper, a painter, & I took pictures of particularly vivid fireplugs, piles piles piles of shit and garbage because I guess they don't clean the city on holiday weekends & due to the absence of people the real peeling state of the East Village was some kind of Sistine Chapel I thought. It was really gorgeous, like «Bye Bye Love».

There's a welter of «you»s in this work, the most poetic being the «I / pick up ‹you› like / my midnight / rattle I shake at the devil / of the night / that does not/scare me... / Quotes always remind me of John Ashbery who practically invented them, I believe. Here I'm addressing my romantic obsession and the gesture or the whole performance of writing a poem.

The easiest you is the «Hot night, wet night / you've seen me before./» Addressing the environment, we know that. Later, «there is sugar / in your coffee / and the band / will catch / you if you/fall.../» This «you» is the poet and, happily, something is reassuring her. Just preceding this the poet had been doing a little dance about whether there was a god or not and resolved that there *was* a «new notebook» and that would have to do. But something does begin to speak to her at at this point, «Make an inventory of / your occupations/.» It functions like a god, a big watcher, and it's doing the addressing now.

After that heightened state things restore themselves to normal, only the «I» is kind of empowered now, challenging. It kind of crows at the you: «You know a / genius when you've / seen one, don't / you. I'm one./ Take a good look, / you've seen me / before. Don't / turn back.../» I think the pronouns have a real wrestling match here, the «I» pushing the you against the wall. A funny moment occurs: «I'm one.» The pronouns merge, the «I» by bullying the you has gathered its forces, is a genius, won't turn back.

«(M)issing you is / not possible in / the New York / rain because / your name / is caught between / the drops.../» is chiefly romantic, talking to the obsession, the gone lover. I guess she's everywhere's there's nothing.

The process of the poem, the performance of it I mentioned, is central to an impression I have that life is a rehearsal for the poem, or the final moment of spiritual revelation. I literally stepped out of my house that night, feeling a poem coming on. Incidentally, it hadn't started raining yet, so I wasn't alone in being ready to burst. I was universally pent up. I had done my research, pretty unconsciously, celebrating the mood I was in. Taking the ferry, watching the Angels, then the explosion of rain and light made it absolutely necessary to go in the deli on 6th street and buy a notebook and pen. I went over to Yaffa and wrote it looking out the window. I haven't changed a thing. The band in the poem is the music in the restaurant and it's their coffee and everything, and naturally I left big tip.

I've had this feeling before—of going out to get a poem, like hunting. The night that comes to mind is the night I wrote the earlier poem. I felt « ...erotic, oddly / magnetic... » like photographic paper. As I walked I was recording the details, I was the details, I was the poem.

I am obsessed with culture. It's my mental community, what configuration of art and art makers I belong with. Alone, I'm the culture of one. I've got my paintings, heroes, cult movies,—any person who lives alone knows the situation of feeling like some kind of private museum. But, I also want to address my culture (some new, larger one out there which I suspect exists) which I begin by making work which violates the hermetic nature of my own museum—as a friendly gesture towards the people who might recognize me. I mean exhibitionistic work, really.

I was in the wreck of one culture the night I was writing this poem. All the monuments lay scattered around: the person I loved, the poet I was ten years ago, the kinds of things that were central then to my life. It's impossible to say anything new about the East Village changing, that wreck, though my most startling experience recently was when I turned a corner on my bike early one evening and didn't recognize any of the stores and didn't know where I was. Even Little Ricky's now asks to check your bag. I walked out angry but I'm sure I'll be back because I've never been able to buy trendy postcards right downstairs before.

—Fall, '87